FLYING WARRIOR

FLYING
WARRIOR

My Life as a
Naval Aviator During
the Vietnam War

JULES HARPER

New York

FLYING WARRIOR
My Life as a Naval Aviator During the Vietnam War

© 2017 **JULES HARPER**

Published in New York, New York, by Morgan James Publishing. Morgan James and The Entrepreneurial Publisher are trademarks of Morgan James, LLC.
www.MorganJamesPublishing.com

The Morgan James Speakers Group can bring authors to your live event. For more information or to book an event visit The Morgan James Speakers Group at www.TheMorganJamesSpeakersGroup.com.

Use of released US Navy imagery does not constitute product or organizational endorsement of any kind by the US Navy.

Shelfie

A **free** eBook edition is available with the purchase of this print book.

CLEARLY PRINT YOUR NAME ABOVE IN UPPER CASE

Instructions to claim your free eBook edition:
1. Download the Shelfie app for Android or iOS
2. Write your name in **UPPER CASE** above
3. Use the Shelfie app to submit a photo
4. Download your eBook to any device

ISBN 978-1-68350-066-7 paperback
ISBN 978-1-68350-067-4 eBook
ISBN 978-1-68350-068-1 hard cover
Library of Congress Control Number:
2016907123

Cover Design by:
Rachel Lopez
www.r2cdesign.com

Interior Design by:
Bonnie Bushman
The Whole Caboodle Graphic Design

In an effort to support local communities, raise awareness and funds, Morgan James Publishing donates a percentage of all book sales for the life of each book to Habitat for Humanity Peninsula and Greater Williamsburg.

Get involved today! Visit
www.MorganJamesBuilds.com

This book is for all the VA-112 personnel who assisted in *Bringing the War to the Enemy*. It is also for my wife, Sandy, daughters, Melissa and Michelle, granddaughters, Avery and Reese, and any future generations so that they will understand my involvement in what occurred off the coast of North Vietnam during the years of 1966–1968.

CONTENTS

ACKNOWLEDGMENTS

I would like to sincerely thank the following people who have assisted me with this manuscript.

A special thanks goes to my family. My wife, Sandy, there from the beginning of my flying journey, was a great help with my spelling, grammar, and editing. Also, my daughter Michelle Allen spent many hours, not only editing but also helping with the technology required to create this manuscript.

I also want to express gratitude to my friends. Mike Hall provided editorial assistance throughout the writing phase and offered inspiring and constructive remarks concerning my writing techniques. Jim Pedersen helped to edit the updated version of the DVD, *Bringing the War to the Enemy*.

I would also like to thank the US Navy for releasing some of the photographs that are displayed in this book.

Preface
BRINGING THE WAR
TO THE ENEMY

Naval aviation played a large role in the Vietnam War that began on August 7, 1964, when the Tonkin Gulf Resolution was passed by Congress. It ended when the last ten marines from our embassy departed Saigon on April 30, 1975. Because of my age and service to the navy, I was involved in this war for two cruises on-board the USS Kitty Hawk as a naval aviator, and my participation was the defining event of my life. I signed and honored a contract with our government to defend our country at all costs.

It has taken me a long time since the war to sit down and record what occurred during this relatively short period of time. After moving into an age fifty-five and over community, I started a Valencia Reserve Veteran's Club and was president for several years. Our club collected donations to erect a flagpole and dedication monument for our community. Each year we have a Veteran's Day party, and all the donations go to the Wounded Warriors of South Florida. They, in turn, pass it on to returning veterans who need temporary assistance adjusting to civilian life.

Shortly after beginning the club, I gave my first presentation on what I experienced in Vietnam, entitled "Bringing the War to the Enemy." This talk also included a sixteen-minute home movie I had filmed while flying missions over Vietnam using a super 8 movie camera. It was so successful that I branched out to give the presentation in other forums, such as local clubs and businesses. It became apparent that there was a large interest in this subject, and I could not do justice to this entire era, which had been a life-changing event for me, in a thirty-minute presentation. That interest is what initially inspired me to write this book. As I continued to write, however, I realized it would be not only a personal account of what had occurred for my family and future family to read, but also a historical account for the general public as well. And finally, in all honesty, it was enjoyable to sit down and relive my past experiences during the navy years.

As a naval aviator flying the A-4 Skyhawk, the backbone of the visual attack bombers used in Vietnam, I feel uniquely qualified to discuss the war. After being a naval aviation cadet for seventeen months, I received my wings and commission in the US Navy on June 25, 1965. The following day, I was married to my wife, Sandy.

Following my initial training in the Replacement Air Group (RAG), flying the A-4C, I deployed for four months on board the USS Forrestal in the Mediterranean. Then, from November, 1966, to June 1, 1968, I did two separate cruises on board the USS Kitty Hawk operating on "Yankee Station" off the coast of North Vietnam. During that time, I flew two hundred combat missions over North and South Vietnam, amassed 332 career carrier take offs and landings, and was awarded the following medals: The Distinguished Flying Cross; Air Medal (Bronze Star for the

First Award); twenty Strike Flight Air Medals; Navy Commendation Medal; Gold Star in lieu of the second Navy Commendation Medal with combat "V"; Navy Achievement Medal; Gold Star in lieu of the second Navy Achievement Medal with combat "V"; Navy Presidential Unit Citation; National Defense Service Medal; Vietnam Service Medal; Vietnam Gallantry Cross Unit Citation; and the Republic of Vietnam Campaign Medal.

As was usual in navy squadrons, I held different collateral jobs during my two cruises besides flying. They included being our squadron's communications officer, navigation officer, airframes and power plant division officer, and the Kitty Hawk's jet engine division officer. My favorite job, however, was holding the position of our squadron's public affairs officer during our second cruise. Part of the responsibility of that job was to send articles about our squadron's twenty-two naval aviators back to the states to be published in local newspapers and used for reports on TV. I managed to keep these articles, along with other pertinent materials, including the Kitty Hawk's cruise yearbook, to help me remember subjects, dates, and details of my two hundred missions flown.

Without the official navy logbook of my flying career, which had been kept by an enlisted yeoman, there would have been no way to correctly describe the details of these missions, which were flown almost fifty years ago. Specifically, the total flight time, aircraft bureau number, and time of day were logged in the record book. The weapons that were carried on each mission were also entered in the logbook, so I had easy access to what ordnance I had delivered on each flight.

Please realize I have tried to be as accurate on all the details as I could, but many years have elapsed. Generally, when the subject is described in the first person, I have thoroughly documented the account of what occurred. When you read the terms, "I remember," or, "I recall," to describe an event, it is my best memory of what transpired but complete documentation was not available. Please note some of the names I have used are aliases for the actual people involved in the story. I have done this to maintain their privacy or because I could not locate them to obtain permission to use their story in this book. And, finally, it is possible that a few details may have slipped away with some of my vanishing brain cells!

History proves that countries have needed warriors throughout the pages of recorded times. People are not born warriors; they have to be trained and given the proper equipment to carry out their missions. Fortunately, we live in a great country, one that is able to assist their future warriors in preparations for battle by supplying them with state-of-the-art equipment. Our warriors are the best in the world, and we better hope they stay that way.

This book does not contain many political statements, even though Vietnam was a huge political arena. As warriors, we would receive our orders from the Commander–in-Chief, the President of the United States. Our military was a "can-do" organization, and we would respond to all orders in a professional manner. Our job was to carry out the president's instructions to the best of our abilities, up to and including the loss of our lives in combat if need be, to successfully complete the mission.

When asked what political party I belong to or what I think about a particular politician, I always respond in the following manner: "I fought in the Vietnam War so you would have the opportunity to talk about your candidate and vote as you see fit. My political thoughts are private."

★ ★ ★ ★ ★

Part I

THE ROAD TO BECOMING A NAVAL AVIATOR

★ ★ ★ ★ ★

Chapter 1

SIXTY-THREE CENTS; BASIC FLIGHT TRAINING

For as long as I can remember, I knew I wanted to be a pilot. My step-father, David Harper, was in the business of heavy construction and supported my desire to become a pilot. I was taught at an early age to respect large mechanical equipment and not be intimidated by its size. When I was approximately twelve years old, David took me out to our local airport and dropped me off to spend the day on my own. I had planned to just visit the various hangers at the field and look at all the airplanes. This kind of freedom and curiosity was allowed at that time.

I wandered into one hanger that had a beautiful, yellow J-3 Cub chocked down in it. The pilot, who was also the owner of the Cub, was doing some work on the inside of the cockpit. We started talking, and I told him I had never been up in an airplane before but really wanted to fly. He asked me how much money I had. I emptied my pockets and counted out sixty-three cents. He said that was plenty to go up and fly around for a while. In those days, things were much simpler.

He finished up his work in the cockpit, and then he strapped me in the front seat of the Cub. He gave me some instructions about what was going to happen during our flight. After starting the engine, we taxied out to the runway and took off. As soon as the wheels left the ground, I knew aviation was what I wanted to do.

As a result of this flight, I built many model airplanes and learned to fly them. During this process, I crashed every one of them until a seasoned modeler taught me the techniques required to fly them successfully. This showed me you have to have instructions to learn how to fly, as a crashed model looks very similar to a real airplane that has crashed.

After two years of college, I made the decision to join the navy in a special program known as the Naval Aviation Cadet Program (NAVCAD). The normal eighteen-month progression provided training in academics, military traditions, physical training, and flying. This program had proven very successful in the past as it allowed not only college graduates to fly but also students with only two years of college. Fleet-enlisted personnel could also join and have a flying career. At the completion of training, the NAVCAD would receive both a reserve commission in the US Navy and his wings.

To begin the process, I had to go to Jacksonville, Florida, and take a physical exam. The team of medical personnel that gave the physicals were reservists, and they only gave them once a month on their active duty weekend. I was doing very well on all the tests—until I took the eye exam. The medical corpsman that administered the test told me I had failed the accommodation portion of the eye test. I asked him what that test meant. He showed me the slide-rule-type instrument he had used to measure my accommodation. He moved the instrument back and forth, showing me where I should have been able to read the letters at my age. I was twenty-years-old at that time and considered myself in excellent health. I had no trouble seeing anything, day or night. The corpsman explained that I would need glasses in the future.

He then told me the test was complete and that I could leave as I was not eligible to continue testing due to failing the eye exam. I began to have a heated discussion with him about the test. It became so loud that the flight surgeon, who was giving a different type of test in the adjoining room, came over and asked what was going on. The corpsman filled him in on the results of my eye test, and the flight surgeon asked him to please leave the room.

The flight surgeon settled me down a little bit and set the accommodation instrument next to me and said he would be back as soon as he finished with the patient in the adjoining room. When he left the room, I picked up the instrument and memorized the letters on it. Shortly, he returned and gave me the test again. This time I passed with flying colors! I continued the rest of the exams, passing them all. My paperwork was signed, and I was given a class date at Pensacola, Florida, to begin my military training. If it hadn't been for that empathetic flight surgeon, I would not have experienced any of the things that were to happen to me in the next few years during my tour of duty.

I continued to fail the accommodation portion of the eye exam every time I had my yearly physical for the navy. Because of my young age, failing this particular exam did not indicate a deficiency in my vision. At age forty-five, however, I went into reading glasses.

I reported to Pensacola, Florida, in February, 1964. During the next seventeen months, I learned a lot about the military and about flying. I also made good friends that would last a life time. After sixteen weeks of basic training, I graduated with my class on May 22, 1964. My class ranking, among my class of twenty-eight, was as follows: first in physical training, third in military bearing, and twelfth in academics.

Even though I was first in physical training, there was one little incident that occurred during the survival water training that should be mentioned. Being from Florida, I grew up loving the water and water sports. I was scuba diving by age fourteen—long before lessons were required to engage in this activity. My roommate, Bruce Bealmear, was a non-swimmer. However, between the navy method of teaching non-swimmers how to swim, which included poking them with a long bamboo pole if their feet touched the bottom of the pool, and my assisting Bruce's practice in our small amount of free time, he became a competent swimmer. While I was helping Bruce, other non-swimming members of my class joined us in the practice sessions. Because of helping them, I had a good reputation for knowing a lot about swimming.

The day came when we had to exhibit our ability to get out of a cockpit that was turned upside down underwater. Crashing into the ocean was simulated as the "cockpit" slid down tracks into the deep end of the pool. The device that was used was called the "Dilbert Dunker." There was a scuba diver standing by in the event of an emergency at the bottom of the pool, watching as the exercise progressed with one student after another taking the ride into the pool on-board the Dilbert Ducker.

Many of my classmates were very apprehensive about doing this required event. I waited to go last as I was counseling several of them, including my friend Bruce, before the plunge. Bruce and my entire class made it through the Dilbert Dunker with no problems. As I climbed into the simulated cockpit, strapping myself in good and tight, I knew I would have no trouble with this ride either.

The instructor made sure I was ready, released the Dilbert Dunker, and then down the rails I went. I remember the cockpit turning upside down and all the air bubbles surrounding me. Slowly and deliberately, I reached down to undo my harness straps, only to find out I could not locate the release mechanism. No problem. I continued to try and locate it—until it became a real problem. I was running out of air at an alarming rate. Panic set in, and shortly after I had swallowed a lot of water, the rescue scuba diver moved in and released me, bringing me to the surface gasping for air.

My classmates watched in amazement as I crawled out of the pool. Sheepishly, I grinned at them as I coughed up what felt like gallons of water. The instructor said, "Ok, sport, get in again, and this time, wait until the air bubbles dissipate before you try and unhook the harness." Down the rails I went again, and heeding the advice of the instructor, I waited for the bubbles to rise up and get out of the way. Reaching down towards the release harness, I found it with no trouble and was soon back up on the side of the pool.

The next stage of training was to go to Saufley Field in Pensacola, join VT-1, the squadron for "primary flight training," and begin the actual flying portion of becoming a naval aviator.

My initial instructor was Lieutenant Harry Watson. On my first flight in the Beechcraft T-34 Mentor, I "tossed my cookies" thirteen times. When we returned to the hanger, I cleaned my flight gloves (where else could I store the vomit in the cockpit of an aircraft?) and was debriefed by Lieutenant Watkins. He assured me that I would not get air sickness anymore. The following day we went flying again, and once more I got sick three times. This time on the debrief, Lieutenant Watkins told me he wasn't sure I was going to be able to "hack the program," due to my airsickness problem. Luckily for me, my desire to become a naval aviator overcame my motion sickness, and I never got airsick again!

I remember one of my early flights with the lieutenant. We had just taken off from Saufley Field, and I was feeling so proud of myself for correctly executing the complicated departure procedure during our climb out. I was talking to him on the aircraft's intercom system about how "wonderful" it felt to be flying. He answered me by saying, "Jules, your departure procedures were great, but we might be able to climb a lot faster if you would raise the gear!" Lieutenant Harry Watson signed my "Certificate of Solo Flight" on July 7, 1964.

My next step in becoming a naval aviator was to go to Whiting Field, Florida, and work my way through VT-2 and VT-3. Here I would learn how to transition into the navy's T-28 Trojan Trainer, which replaced the former trainer aircraft, the venerable SNJ. Learning precision, acrobatics, basic instruments, radio instruments, formation flying, night flying, and, of course, sixteen more weeks of ground school was the syllabus.

The T-28 was a beautiful aircraft to fly. It was built by North American Aviation and was powered by a 1425HP engine, known as a Wright R-1820-9 radial engine. There were two models of the aircraft. One was the T-28B, 489 built, which did not have a tail hook, and the T-28C, 266 built, which did have a tail hook. The Charlie model had a shorter propeller for use when landing on an aircraft carrier. The Bravo flew more smoothly, quickly, and quietly than did the Charlie.

When you started the engine, it coughed, belched white smoke, and was very noisy. Because the engine was so large and developed so much torque, the pilot had to apply a lot of right rudder during acceleration to keep the plane going straight during takeoff. One of the stories I heard at Whiting Field concerned a T-28B that ran off the left side of the runway during takeoff. The student pilot who was flying the aircraft was a Naval Academy graduate under the direction of his instructor.

During the accident investigation, as the story went, the instructor stated he said repeatedly to the student, "Add more right rudder, right rudder, right rudder." The student answered, "I am! I am!" When the board asked the Naval Academy graduate why he didn't follow his instructor's advice, he said, "Sir, I got my left foot confused with my right foot."

Following VT-2 and VT-3 at Whiting Field, I moved back to Saufley Field to join VT-5. Here I learned the concepts of landing an airplane on an aircraft carrier. In February, 1965, my instructor and I flew out to the USS Wasp, which was the training carrier operating off the coast of Jacksonville, Florida, at that time. I was sitting in the back seat of the T-28 as we came aboard the ship. No problem until the instructor, following the lineman's signals, taxied the aircraft over to the side of the carrier to be parked. I looked out of the cockpit and into the moving Atlantic Ocean, some eighty feet below, and almost "tossed my cookies" again. Fortunately, I managed to get out of the aircraft and away from the side of the flight deck! Aircraft carriers, a new concept to me, would become my home in less than a year.

Chapter 2

BENDING THE RULES; ADVANCED FLIGHT TRAINING; MARRIAGE

After basic training flying the T-34 and T28, my orders read something like this: "Report to Corpus Christi, VT-31, to fly the T-44A Tracker." The T-44A was a twin-engine, propeller-driven aircraft known as the "Stoof." The Stoof was used primarily as an anti-submarine aircraft. Its secondary mission was to act as a carrier on-board delivery (COD) aircraft. In its secondary role, it brought passengers, cargo, and mail to the carrier while it was at sea.

As nice of an airplane as the Stoof was, I wanted to fly jets. I arrived in Corpus early, and it was a weekend. The officer of the day called me in and said I didn't need to be there until the following Friday. He said he did not have any orders for me at that time. I told him I knew that, but that I had been instructed to report early to start the jet class in Kingsville, Texas, on Monday, which was not exactly true. After some discussion, he stamped what paperwork I had and said, "Ok, son, get down there to Kingsville and fly those 'Stove Pipes.'" Thanks to Navy bureaucracy, by the time my "real orders" reached Kingsville, I was already established in the jet training syllabus, and nothing was ever said about it. That's how I became a jet pilot!

I checked into VT-21 at Kingsville, Texas, in the month of February, 1965. One very interesting event that happened during my training was when our class of ten students went out to the "line" to demonstrate that we knew the correct procedures to pre-flight the TF-9J Cougar jet. This plane was the replacement for the old Panther jet, which was a straight-wing fighter used in Korea, and the Cougar was the first jet I was to fly.

Besides kicking the tires, looking for hydraulic leaks, etc., we also had to climb up on the wing, walk to the fuselage area, and push open the two "blow-in doors," which provided air to the engine at slow speeds. We could then look down into the inside of the fuselage where the engine was located and check it for damage. One of our classmates smoked cigarettes, and we were wearing our flight suits, which had a lot of pockets. As he bent over to look into the engine area, a cigarette lighter fell out of one of his open pockets and landed somewhere in the engine compartment. It took the maintenance division several days to pull the fuselage apart and search the engine for the lighter. After an extensive search, the lighter was found, and the jet was put back together. The student received a "down," which meant he had to repeat this particular event before moving on. It was pointed out to all of our classmates that we were in an occupation that required constant "attention to detail" to keep us alive! Point well taken.

Before we actually flew the jet, we had to go back out to the "line" (where the aircraft were parked) and start the engine in the F-9. After flying the T-28, which was very exciting every time you started the engine, the F-9 just made a little bit of a "whine sound," and you had to look at the instruments to make sure it was running and idling at the correct rpm.

The day finally came when I got to actually fly the plane with the first of several instructors I was to experience, Marine Captain Tim (Mad Dog) Mason. Whatever the jet lacked in starting excitement, it made up for it with its speed. The first time I accelerated down the runway for takeoff, the plane reached a speed of 140 knots; it soon rotated and became airborne. I had been used to flying the T-28, which cruised at a speed a little less than two hundred knots. The F-9 had a top speed of 562 knots and cruised at about three hundred and fifty knots. It took a while flying at these speeds to be able to get your thinking process "up to speed" to identify objects on the ground and thus stay ahead of the aircraft. It always amazed me at how well one's mind could adapt to do this.

In May, 1965, I was introduced to an event that was really exciting. I was flying a "Hop," as we called them, when, out of nowhere, another F-9 flew right below us at a higher rate of speed and pulled up directly in front of our nose! We flew through the "jet wash" and were physically shaken in the aircraft. My instructor called out on the common radio frequency, which we all monitored: "If it's war you want, its war you get!" We then began to "hassle" with not only the F-9 that had attacked us but also with several other aircraft that had joined the fray. "Hassle" is another word for air-to-air combat. The idea is to position your aircraft behind another plane (six o'clock position) and simulate shooting it down. It is tremendously competitive and requires great flying ability to "win the match."

This situation was strictly forbidden at our stage of training, but it sometimes occurred. The reason that it was not allowed was because you cannot see all the aircraft that are involved in the "fight." This can lead (and has led) to two or more airplanes running into each other with disastrous results. This brings up a crucial aviation rule: "Never allow two aircraft to occupy the same airspace at the same time."

The reason that the hassling rule is broken occasionally is because "hassling is as much fun as you can have with your clothes on!" Needless to say, I was hooked on it from then on and was never beaten in a "hassle" during my entire navy career.

April 19, 1965, I soloed in an AF-9J jet fighter (single-seat version of the TF-9). It's bureau number was 140145, and it was a sharp little aircraft. The flight time was just short of an hour and a half and was one of the high points in my training up to that point.

On May 10th, I began my field carrier landing practice (FCLP) flights to get ready to do carrier qualifications prior to finishing my training. This event was handled by a qualified landing signaling officer (LSO). He stationed himself at the end of the "duty runway," as it was called. It was the runway used for take offs and landings. It was his job to watch the student pilots fly the glide slope down to the field and make a touch-and-go landing. If a pilot was deviating from the glide slope, he would make a radio call and tell him to correct his rate of descent. Some of his calls could have been, "You're high; you're low; power; go around; the deck is pitching; don't chase the meatball; divert." A touch and go is when the aircraft touches the ground and the pilot moves a switch to restore the speed brakes to the stored position, adds full power to the engine, and takes off again to continue practicing his landings. This simulates the same procedure the pilot would use while operating on an aircraft carrier. At the end of the training session, the LSO would debrief each pilot, explaining what he did right and what he did wrong.

This exercise was practiced using a gyroscopically controlled concave mirror, known as Fresnel lens optical landing system (FLOLS), located on the port side of the carrier's flight deck. It showed the pilots the correct glide slope by using a yellow "meatball" or "ball," as it is called, located in between two sets of green lights called "datum lights."

This whole set of lights was gyroscopically controlled. It compensated for a lot of the movement of the flight deck caused by rough sea conditions. The pilot had to adjust his aircraft's rate of descent to keep the meatball right in the middle of the datum lights. If the meatball went above the green datum lights, the pilot was high on the glide slope. If the meatball went below the green datum lights, he was low on the glide slope. By keeping the meatball right in the middle of the two sets of green lights, the pilot would land on the aircraft carrier in a position to catch the number three "target" wire.

An aircraft carrier has four raised wires that stretch across its angled flight deck. The number one wire is closest to the "fantail" (aft position on the flight deck). The number two, three, and four wires move forward from the number one wire so as to provide a landing area that the aircraft can touch down on and catch one of them using its tail hook. It sounds simple, but the tail hook, which is located on the lower fuselage in the aft section of the plane, can hit the flight deck and jump or skip across the wires, creating a "bolter" situation. When this happened, the LSO would say to the pilot over the radio, "Bolter, bolter, power, and go." The pilot would then add full power on the engine, retract the speed brake, and take off to come back and try to land aboard the ship again.

When May 21, 1965, arrived, I found myself out in the Gulf of Mexico on board the USS Lexington, CVS-16. During my first catapult shot—the catapult launches the aircraft off the flight deck—I was required to salute the flight deck officer, giving the signal for him to fire the catapult. I was nervous and did not want to take my right hand off the control stick to do this. After a short delay, the air boss, who oversaw all flight deck operations, came over the radio and said, "He's not going to launch you until you salute." I saluted, and about three seconds later, I was flying off the carrier. I repeated this procedure four more times, saluting for each cat shot, and logged five carrier landings in the Cougar that day.

I continued to fly a total of 114 hours in the F-9 before moving on to my final training squadron, VT-23, where we learned to fly the Tiger jet.

VT-23 was a training squadron in Kingsville, Texas, that flew the supersonic Grumman F-11A Tiger jet used by the Blue Angels from 1957–1969. This plane was designed using the new concept (at that time) of "area rule," which means the fuselage looked a lot like an old glass coke bottle. The coke-bottle shape reduced transonic drag, making it perform much better at supersonic speeds.

The Tiger had the unique distinction of being the first aircraft to ever shoot itself down. In 1956, during flight testing, the pilot put the F-11 into a shallow dive and fired the 20mm cannons. As the trajectory of the bullets decayed, they crossed path with the Tiger jet, hitting it several times and causing it to crash. The pilot survived, but the plane was destroyed.

Learning about all this in training, flying was to become even more fun! There were no two-seat versions of the Tiger. For this reason, the training squadron wanted to make sure you knew everything you needed to know before they sent you out on your first "hop." Not only did you have to know the purpose of every switch in the cockpit, you also had to be able to locate them blindfolded and turn them on or off as needed. We had already been tested on how the ejection seat worked while flying the F-9, but we had to go through the procedures on how to eject from the F-11 as it was a little different.

On June 5, 1965, flying an F-11, bureau number 141876, I flew my first hop from Kingsville, followed by my instructor chase pilot flying another F-11. The flight lasted one hour and twelve minutes. It was drilled into our heads during training that "you will not go supersonic anywhere you want to." This was obviously to avoid damaging buildings, etc. on the ground with the shockwave the aircraft produced when it broke the sound barrier. Two days later, I flew supersonic for the first time in the Tiger jet! The only way I could tell I was traveling faster than the speed of sound was to look at the airspeed/Mach indicator and see it pass through 1.0 and continue up to almost 1.2 Mach.

On June 9, 1965, I flew the Tiger for one hour and thirty-six minutes without my chase pilot escorting me. It was an afternoon flight, and there were a few large, towering cumulus nimbus clouds in the area. Those are the really big ones that you see in bad rain storms. We had been instructed to never fly through one of them as it could destroy the aircraft due to turbulence and large pieces of hail.

I flew up to an altitude of fifty thousand feet. This was as high as you were authorized to fly without wearing a "pressure suit." If you went any higher and the aircraft were to lose cabin pressurization, your blood would boil, and you would die instantly. As I pushed the control stick forward to begin my descent, I was heading in the direction of one of those cumulus nimbus clouds. I continued in its direction, and passing through about twenty thousand feet, I began to pull back on the control stick and "ran" straight up the side of this huge cloud. I lit the afterburner and continued to climb upward until I came to the top of the storm cloud, which was around thirty-five thousand feet. I then rolled upside down and pulled back on the control stick to fly right over the top of this beauty with lightning flashing beneath me. When I reached the other side, I lowered the nose of the jet, reduced the power, and flew back down to twenty thousand feet as I started thinking to myself about what power this aircraft had and what a feeling of complete freedom it gave.

June 11, 1965, was the day some of us were to demonstrate our ability in the high altitude gunnery pattern. The flight consisted of six jets. The first pilot was an instructor who pulled the target "banner." The next flight of four F-11s, known as a division, were all students. We were being followed by our chase instructor pilot.

We had all been briefed on how to attack this "towed target banner." We would roll in one at a time from an altitude of about thirty-five thousand feet and come screaming down at a high rate of speed, lock our gun-sights on the banner, and begin firing live ammunition at the target. Each of our 20mm cannons had different colored bullets, which later would determine the number of hits made by each pilot in the banner.

The one thing that had been stressed by our instructor was, "Make damn sure you have the aircraft ahead of you in sight and be sure he has pulled off the target before you begin to fire." The flight was going right on schedule, and I was getting ready to attack the banner. I rolled in shortly after my wingman and began to fire my 20mm cannons at the target. Shortly after I had pulled the trigger, the F-11 ahead of me pulled up from the target, and it looked to me as if he ran right through my 20mm bullets! At the same time, he tried to light his afterburner to accelerate the Tiger and climb back to a higher altitude. It did not light; instead it sent raw fuel out the exhaust pipe, and at that altitude and due to the temperature, it appeared to me as "smoke." I thought to myself, *Oh, my God, I've shot my wingman down!* Fortunately for all concerned, I did not put any bullets in his plane—or in the target banner!

June 16th was to be a flight to practice acrobatics and air-to-air combat (hassling). I took off, followed by my instructor, and climbed to fifteen thousand feet and headed to the practice area. The first maneuver to practice was a "loop," which I had done many times in previous aircraft operating at a slower airspeed.

I began the maneuver by reaching the required airspeed of 480 knots. I pulled back on the stick hard enough to put four g's (four times the normal one g on earth) on the aircraft. The F-11 manual said to hold these g's until you complete the loop. Somewhere near the top of the loop, I released some of the back stick pressure, thereby reducing the g's, and found myself going straight up. It didn't take long to begin to run out of airspeed, so I attempted to light the afterburner for more power. It did not light. So there I was at thirty thousand feet, streaming fuel out of the back of the aircraft, getting low on airspeed at an alarming rate, and running out of ideas all at the same time. The aircraft rate of climb stopped, and I went into the beginning of a spin. My instructor took one look at this mess and screamed, "Harper, what the hell are you doing?" I regained control of the aircraft and soon we began to hassle. After a few minutes of air-to-air combat, my instructor, already irritated with me, screamed into the radio again, "Harper, where are you now?" I answered, "Check your six o'clock!"

On June 21, 1965, I flew my last flight in the Tiger. I had flown many hassle sorties against my instructors in this short period of time and never lost a single one. My flight grades were average in most areas but always excellent in the area of air-to-air combat. I had logged 24.7 hours of flight time in this beautiful Tiger jet, and my desire to be a fighter pilot was reinforced.

When you get near to completing your flight training, the navy requires you to fill out a form requesting what type of aircraft you want to fly in the fleet and where you want to be based. I had put in to fly jet fighters, specifically, the Phantom jet based in Jacksonville, Florida.

When my orders came through, they read something like this: "Due to the conflict in Vietnam, you and your entire class are assigned to fly the A-4, Skyhawk, based in Lemoore, California." The Skyhawk was an attack aircraft and much slower than a jet fighter. This was a situation where navy bureaucracy and karma worked against me to provide for "the needs of the service," which I was just beginning to learn about!

June 25, 1965, was the day ten of my classmates, including myself, received our wings. Because I had been in the NAVCAD program, I also received my commission as an ensign in the United States Navy Reserve on that same day.

As I had mentioned earlier, in the NAVCAD program you could not be married. You had to be a commissioned officer to be married. One of my NAVCAD classmates had been "secretly married" for the nineteen months it took him to reach this point in becoming a naval aviator. Had he been killed in training, his wife would not have received any navy benefits, which included ten thousand dollars available to officers in that program. It was a big day for both he and his wife, and they really celebrated! Unfortunately, within six months, at the Chocolate Mountain Aerial Gunnery range located in California, he was killed. He was performing a dive bombing run, flying an A-4C Skyhawk, and ran into the ground after dropping his bombs. Throughout our training program, we had lost several pilots, but this one was especially hard on all of us. He had finally gotten "legal" to be married, and it was just a darn shame.

After being engaged for over seventeen months, on June 26, 1965, Sandy Gilley and I were married in a full military wedding at Kingsville, Texas. We had a few of our relatives and numerous classmates of mine in attendance. There were enough navy and marine classmates dressed in their formal military whites acting as ushers that we were able to assemble them outside the chapel and walk under their crossed swords, or arch of swords as it was also known. This tradition was meant to ensure the couple's safe passage into their new life together. Keeping with military tradition, we used my saber to cut our wedding cake at the reception. (In 2015, we used it again to cut our fiftieth-anniversary cake.)

In Texas, the month of June is very hot. I had been driving a VW Bug that did not have air conditioning. Sandy's parents exchanged cars with us so we could have their air conditioned Chevrolet while driving on our honeymoon to New Orleans, where they lived at the time. God bless them for switching. We were in route to my first duty assignment, which was in Millington, Tennessee. After staying there one month, we would move on to Lemoore, California.

It took us five days just to get to New Orleans, which is normally a two-day trip at the most. We were to exchange cars again with Sandy's folks to continue our trip to Millington. As you can imagine, we just couldn't pass up the nice-looking motels on our way to New Orleans. Sandy's dad told us as we were leaving their house that if we continued at that pace of travel, going from Millington to Lemoore, my tour of duty in the navy might be over by the time we got there!

Heeding his warning, we arrived in Millington in time for me to start the classes in Power plant and Airframes. Right on schedule, I graduated from both these schools, prepared to become the officer in charge of all the jet engines on board the USS Kitty Hawk during my future second cruise.

Traveling to California, we were dragging a small U-Haul trailer behind us, filled with all our worldly possessions. We were also learning to deal with a young German Sheppard puppy we had adopted from a friend along the way. We named her "Happy." She was a real nice addition to our new family.

We spent one delightful night in Estes Park, Colorado, where I had stayed with my grandparents many years before. It was interesting to me as almost everything appeared to be just as I had remembered it with them. Crossing the Continental Divide, we got caught in a severe snow storm that I thought was as dangerous as any flying I had done up to that time. Because my windshield wipers did not work on the VW, I had to use my left arm, holding the wiper blade, to clear the driver's window of snow so I could see.

The rest of the trip to California was uneventful until we got to the town of Lemoore. We stopped at a gas station on a small street with multiple little shops on each side of the road and asked the attendant where the town was. He replied, "This is the main street." I looked over at Sandy, and she had started to cry. The attendant went on to say the base was thirteen miles farther to the west and had a much larger population. After living in a couple of rentals near town for a few months, we moved onto the base and enjoyed government quarters and the camaraderie of living close to other naval aviators and their families.

Chapter 3
THE RAG; JOINING VA-112

I t turns out the navy does things a little differently than the rest of the world. For example, the navy calls the floor a deck; a wall is called a bulkhead; the ceiling is called an overhead; the bathroom is called a head; a drinking fountain is called a scuttlebutt; and the hallway is called a passageway. The most commonly known exceptions are right is starboard and left is port. I had a good air force friend years later tell me, "Jules, you navy guys are so prim and proper. You say, come starboard five degrees, come port seven degrees, but let you get into trouble, and its right full rudder!" I had to agree with him.

A spear has been used as a weapon for thousands of years by warriors all around the world. Take the head of the spear for this analogy of all the branches of the US Military Services. Place all the different branches in the spear's head, depending on the job and particular service. The closer one is to combat, the closer to the point of the spear he would be placed.

For example, my step father was in the army and stationed in the Dallas/Fort Worth area, helping to manage a military golf course for his tour of duty. In this example, he would be placed towards the rear of the spearhead. If you were in the supply division of your branch of the service, you would probably be closer to the point of the spear.

The tip of the spear is reserved for the warriors. A warrior is defined as the person who delivers the weapons directly on the enemy 24/7. Who throws this spear in today's environment? The answer, ever since the Korean Conflict, has been the Commander-in-Chief, or the President of the United States.

The decade of the sixties was the decade President Kennedy was assassinated, the Beatles arrived in our country, and the Vietnam War was heating up. We were also involved in a terrible cold war with Russia that, fortunately, we all lived through.

Vietnam in wartime is where I found myself, along with the other twenty-one naval aviators in our squadron, from November, 1966, through June, 1968. With the exception of a short, four-month deployment to the Mediterranean on board the USS Forrestal, my life was centered directly on the tip of the spear.

VA 125 was the Replacement Air Group (RAG) located in Lemoore, California, and it was there that we transitioned into the A-4 Skyhawk. One of the first few days I was at the squadron, there was a meeting for all the new naval aviators. The squadron officer told us that no matter what was going on over in Vietnam, our primary mission was that of being a nuclear weapons delivery pilot.

He went on to say, "Here in the RAG, we will be trained to carry out that mission, plus conventional weapon delivery." We had all been given top-secret clearances, and we were asked if we would have trouble dropping a nuclear weapon on a military target that was close to a city, possibly killing thousands of people. The unanimous answer was no; we would all do it. We had just finished training, and even though we were in our early twenties, we knew what our responsibilities were. Had any of us said no, I imagine he would have been reassigned to a different type of aircraft. The officer then began to tell us what would be expected of us. As I recall, he gave us three scenarios in the event of a nuclear war.

"The first scenario is each of you will take off from the carrier in your A-4 and climb to altitude following procedures that will be discussed later. You will then descend to an altitude that will allow you to avoid being detected by enemy radar, proceed to the initial point (IP) at a low altitude of fifty feet, turn to the pre-selected heading, fly to the release point for the nuclear weapon, and release it. At that time, you will fly away from the target area and return to the ship."

After he took a breath, he continued: "There are two problems with this scenario. The first one is you probably will not have enough fuel to make it back to the carrier. The second problem is that the useful life expectancy of an aircraft carrier in a nuclear war is about twenty minutes. The ship would be hit with a nuclear weapon delivered by a missile.

"The second scenario is the same as the first, except, instead of returning to the ship, you will proceed to a friendly nation. The trouble with this scenario is, even if you could make it there with the fuel you have on board, the friendly country would already be getting hit with nuclear weapons because they are friendly with the United States.

"That brings us to the third and most-probable scenario. You do the same procedure as mentioned above with one exception. After delivering your weapon, you fly about fifty miles away from your target area and eject. You might want to brush up on your Russian language skills as you will be talking with the Russians for a long time."

At this time, one of our new naval aviators raised his hand to ask a question. "Sir, it seems to me that since we have heard our targets are going to also be hit with an ICBM, Polaris Missile, and another aircraft flown by the air force, a smarter scenario might be this: Take off from the carrier. When you are out of sight of the ship, pickle off your nuclear weapon on "safe," sending it harmlessly to the bottom of the ocean, and turn to a heading that will get you to a nice, remote island, like, say, Tahiti! There you could live happily ever after." Never let it be said that naval aviators don't have a sense of humor!

Our instructor officer shook his head and continued: "You're A-4 is basically a throw-away nuclear bomber. To give you the best opportunities to complete your mission successfully, the aircraft has been equipped with a clamshell-type internal canopy. You can pull it forward, and it will keep the flash of nuclear weapons that have been detonated in your general area from blinding you when you are at high altitude.

"You will also be wearing a gold faceplate visor on your helmet, like the astronaut's wear, and you will want to obtain an eye patch, like the old pirates used, to keep one eye covered in case the flash from a nuclear bomb blinds your other eye.

"There will be much more about this subject as you proceed with your transitional training in the A-4. Right now, just work your butts off studying so you won't kill yourselves when you begin flying this aircraft. Good day, gentlemen."

I remember my first flight in the Skyhawk, accelerating down the runway, gaining speed to take off. There was no after burner on the A-4, so it accelerated more slowly and was not as spectacular as the F-11 had been. It was an easy airplane to fly, although it was not as stable flying formation as the F-11.

Besides learning to fly the new aircraft, we learned how to prepare the missions to attack our nuclear target. Once we knew where our target was located, we brought our large area charts and glued them together so the entire route was covered. We used a green magic marker to draw in the route we planned to fly on these charts. We also drew in anything else that would be helpful for us to know. Examples of this would be navigation information on the green line, anti-aircraft weapons, missile sites, or some outstanding geographical area that would help us visually navigate.

Then we cut "strip charts" that we neatly folded to fit on our map holder located on our left leg. A strip chart was approximately eight inches in width and twelve inches in length, and the green navigation line was right in the middle of it. We continued to spend two weeks in between each of our cruises doing this same process. This insured our charts were up to date with any new information that was available—even though we would be fighting a conventional war in Vietnam.

Our aircraft radar was used to pick out significant geographical points along with the clock on the airplane using time/distance to verify our position. Most amazingly, once again we learned to speed up our thinking processes flying at this low altitude of fifty feet so we could comfortably see and identify items on the ground around us while cruising at 352 knots.

There were specified low-altitude routes on the courses in California we flew over. As a result of seeing all the natural beauty while doing this, we got to appreciate the state of California even more.

The navy had a special area in which we could practice our air-to-air combat skills with one another. It was located east of Lemoore and extended over the Sierra Nevada Mountains. One of our classmates was on a hop, hassling another A-4 in this area, when he lost control of his airplane and went into a spin at an altitude of about twenty-five thousand feet. It was a cloudy day at the lower altitudes, and he went into the clouds. He later told me, "Jules, all of a sudden, I knew I wanted to get out of that airplane more than anything in the world. I pulled down the 'face curtain,' which started the ejection sequence, and found myself outside the aircraft falling through space. My parachute opened, and a split second later I stepped on ground! Talk about a close call!" As a result of this accident and his desire to change his assignment of flying jets, he was reassigned to fly helicopters. He figured his number was up flying jets, and you must volunteer to fly as a naval aviator.

Another interesting accident concerning ejecting out of an A-4 over the high Sierra Nevada Mountains had occurred prior to my arrival. The pressure-sensing device was set to open the parachute at an altitude of ten thousand feet. When the naval aviator had ejected, he landed in a deep snow drift near Mount Whitney, without his parachute opening. Mount Whitney is over fourteen thousand feet in elevation, with the surrounding mountain range well above ten thousand feet.

When the rescue team arrived, they were amazed that he had survived the free fall into the snow drift. Taking him down the mountain with all his gear, including most of the ejection seat, the pressure-sensing device set off the opening sequence of the parachute in the back of the truck as they passed ten thousand feet, surprising everyone!

While I was in the RAG, I assumed, like all of my classmates, I would be going to Vietnam. Two weeks before I finished my training, my orders were changed to join Attack Squadron 112. VA-112 was a West Coast Squadron on "exchange duty" with an East Coast Squadron operating in the Mediterranean area on board the USS Forrestal.

At the time, I thought, due to the needs of the service, how fortunate I was to be going to the Mediterranean area for four months instead of to Vietnam. Time would prove this thought to be incorrect as Russia and China were adding, each and every day, huge amounts of armament in the form of anti-aircraft weapons and surface-to–air (SAM) missiles to fortify Vietnam. Needless to say, by the time I got there later in the year, it was much more heavily defended than it would have been earlier.

I was being sent to VA-112 to replace Lt. Bob Johnson, a naval aviator who had been killed. Following a successful carrier landing, he was taxiing out of the arresting cable that stopped his aircraft when he noticed that his brakes were not working. As he moved forward on the flight deck, he was heading towards the starboard elevator, which was down some sixty feet at the time. The A-4 that he was flying did not have nose-wheel steering and relied on differential braking to steer the aircraft. Prior to going over the edge of the flight deck, he ejected out of the A-4. Unfortunately, the giant Tillie crane was located just forward of the carrier's island. The Tillie crane resembles a dragline type of equipment with a large boom. It was used to move disabled aircraft from one place to another in times of emergencies.

As the ejection seat and Bob were traveling upward, being propelled by a rocket motor, they struck the Tillie crane, cutting Bob in half. His legs remained on the flight deck while the top part of his body went into the Mediterranean Sea. As a result of this accident, the Tillie crane on all carriers was moved to a position behind the carrier's island to be out of the way.

It turned out that another naval aviator finishing the RAG had orders to join VA-112. Alexander Palenscar, a Naval Academy graduate, known to everyone as "Doc," was replacing LTJG John Cummins. John had been killed practicing a night bombing run on a target being dragged by one of our destroyers in the Mediterranean Sea. After he had dropped his practice bombs on the target, he failed to pull out from his dive and crashed into the sea.

"Doc" and I left in January, 1966, traveling over to Naples, Italy, to join our squadron aboard the USS Forrestal. We had a week in Naples, and we took advantage of the time to visit museums and other local attractions. The high point for me was visiting the ruins of Pompeii and the Mount Vesuvius Volcano Crater. At the time, you could walk part way down into the crater and imagine the disaster that was caused when this volcano had erupted. Getting the chance to see sights like these was one of the perks of being in the navy.

VA-112's history began in 1944. Formed as a fighter bomber squadron, it flew the F6F Grumman Hellcat during World War II. After transitioning to the F8F Bearcats, which like the Hellcat was a pre-jet aircraft, VF-112 made one of the initial post war cruises around the world in 1948 aboard the USS Valley Forge.

In January 1950, after a quick transition to the F9F-2B Grumman Panther jet aircraft, the squadron departed for Korea aboard the USS Philippine Sea. Fighting 112 compiled an impressive combat record. Its engagements included providing major air cover during the retreat from the Chosen Reservoir, the Inchon invasion, and the Wonson landings. Only the signing of the Korean truce prevented a third combat tour for the squadron as it was already steaming for Korea aboard the USS Kearsearge.

With peace restored, the squadron returned to the United States in September, 1953, switched to the F9F-6 Cougar from the Panther, and returned to the Far East with the USS Kearsearge. With the completion of this tour, VF-112 bid a fond goodbye to the USS Kearsearge and greeted a newer, improved version of the Cougar, the F9F-8. In short order, the squadron demonstrated its outstanding ability to master any new aircraft by winning the Navy Weapons Meet at El Centro, California, in 1956. Then VF-112 departed to the Far East once again, this time aboard the USS Essex.

In 1957, the squadron received the McDonnell F3H-2M Demon, also known as the widow maker. It was a very difficult aircraft to fly, and many naval aviators were killed flying it. In August of 1958, the squadron returned for its third cruise to the Far East aboard the USS Ticonderoga.

In March, 1959, the old bowed out and the new bowed in as the name VF "Fighting" 112 was relegated to an honored position in the naval air history books. With a new mission and new aircraft, the squadron was designated Attack Squadron 112 and commenced training in the Douglas A4D Skyhawk. With the other units of CVG-11, VA-112 deployed to the Western Pacific (Wes Pac) in July 1960 and enjoyed a highly successful eight-month cruise aboard the USS Hancock. VA-112 returned to NAS Miramar to receive an improved version of their aircraft called the A4D-2N. In later years, this aircraft's designation was changed to the A-4C Skyhawk, nicknamed the "scooter" because of its small size.

After nine years at NAS Miramar, the Broncos, using a call sign of Montana, received word to move to a newly constructed base at Lemoore, California. The cross section of the terrain surrounding the new base contained geographical similarities to any trouble area in the world, and NAS Lemoore soon became the scene of extensive training for VA-112 to ready them for any contingency.

After two subsequent deployments to Wes Pac, which terminated in July of 1964, the Broncos were praised by Commander Fleet Air Hawaii as the "Best Weapons System" observed that year. The squadron went on to win the Commander Fleet Air Alameda "Ready Strike IV" exercise in competition with six other squadrons by demonstrating its ability to execute an attack on an unfamiliar target with conventional weapons.

In July 1965, the squadron deployed from the East Coast aboard the USS Forrestal, along with Carrier Air Wing Eight, bound for the Mediterranean Sea.

VA-112 had been cruising on-board the Forrestal for over five months when Doc and I checked aboard in Naples. It turned out that no officer in the squadron could ever remember having a naval aviator with the rank of ensign arrive during their cruise. Apparently, there were not that many NAVCAD graduates, and most arriving new naval aviators at least held the rank of lieutenant junior grade (LTJG). So my inexperience was a real rarity!

I was assigned a "big brother" by the name of Lt. Phil Sisney to help me get acclimated to shipboard life. What I didn't realize was that during the previous few weeks before Doc and I arrived, my future squadron mates were preparing a "special welcome" for me.

Phil told me a responsibility of the communications officer, to which I had been assigned, was to keep a logbook on the teletype machine that came in each day. The tape was about one half inch wide and ran for as long as the message continued. He explained to me the commanding officer read the "ticker tapes" daily, and it really helped him to have it all sorted out and put neatly into a logbook.

This sounded very logical to me as a naïve, dedicated, motivated, career-oriented new member of the squadron. Each day I would get out my glue and go to work placing all the tapes in exact order into a folder so our skipper could speed read through them. Of course, all of this was just busy work that was humorous to the other officers of the squadron. Our skipper was just as much involved in this prank as the rest of the pranksters. As it turned out, this was just a preview to the really big joke they pulled on me.

After we left the Port of Naples, we were heading to Barcelona, Spain, conducting flight operations along the way. We had been at sea for about a week when my big brother Phil told me the skipper wanted me to stand the "mail buoy watch." I told Phil I did not know what this watch entailed. He slowly explained what my responsibilities were to be: "Jules, in the history of the navy, during at-sea conditions, which we are now in, sensitive mail is dropped from a low-flying aircraft near the carrier and is picked up by an at-sea detail of enlisted men using the carrier's dinghy. Your job is to stand a four-hour watch, which is really simple. You just proceed to the portside bow area of the carrier and keep an eye open for when the aircraft drops the mail buoy into the sea and then tell the air boss where it has landed."

On the misty, cold, rainy, designated day, at noon, wearing my leather flight jacket, I proceeded to the bow of the carrier to stand my watch. Obviously, I did not know TV cameras were focused on me or that I could be seen on screen throughout the ship.

After about an hour, the rain began to come down harder. I was already grounded due to a cold. I began to think that this was a stupid watch and marched myself up to where the air boss was on duty. I addressed him with a sharp salute and began to explain that I didn't think, as a naval aviator, I should be out there on the flight deck, in the rain, standing this watch. Keeping his military bearing, with serious face he told me to go down and talk to my skipper. Arriving in the squadron's ready room, I found every naval aviator of our squadron—including the skipper—viewing our TV and laughing hysterically while watching reruns of me standing the "mail buoy watch" on the flight deck!

Chapter 4
RUSSIAN PLANES; LOSS OF A SQUADRON MATE

In the Port of Barcelona, we anchored out in the bay, our normal procedure in case we had to leave quickly. An A-4 Skyhawk equipped with a Mk 43 nuclear weapon was set up on the flight deck, with two marine guards around it at all times, to be viewed by visiting dignitaries. Military protocol dictates two people are required to be around a nuclear weapon to cut down the chances of planned sabotage or some other adverse act.

During this period of time, we were still deeply involved in a cold war with Russia. Part of our job was to show the world that we had assets that could be used if the cold war ever turned hot. The visiting dignitaries were told that this Skyhawk could be launched in less than ten minutes, if need be, by cutting the anchor chain and getting the carrier underway. The Skyhawk would then be launched to its pre-selected target.

During each cruise to the Mediterranean Sea, our carriers were always visited by a Russian Bear nuclear bomber that flew over us to prove they could attack at any time. Our F-8 Crusaders and F-4 Phantom fighter jets would intercept them at exactly two hundred miles away from the carrier during each of their visits. We did not want the Russians to know our actual capabilities of intercepting them before this point. As a matter of fact, our ship knew when they took off from a Russian airport, thanks to a sophisticated spy network we had in place that would have made the intercept point much farther away from our ships.

As the Russian airplane flew over our carrier's position, all the crewmen on the flight deck stopped whatever they had been doing to wave at the plane. Our fighters who were accompanying the bomber said the Russian crew members were waving back at our men. It all seemed very surreal.

In the US Navy, for the flight deck crew to receive monthly flight-deck hazardous duty pay, the aircraft carrier had to conduct flight operations at least one day during that month. On April 1, 1966 (April fool's day), the USS Forrestal conducted one day of flight operations to fulfill this requirement as they were steaming east to return to CONUS (Continental United States). One of our squadron naval aviators completed his pre-flight checks of his A-4 and, shortly afterwards, was launched off one of the waist (aft) catapults.

As the Skyhawk cleared the flight deck, it began to roll uncontrollably to the port. Passing through about one hundred degrees of left bank, the pilot "punched out" (ejected out) of the A-4. By the time the ejection seat had cleared the aircraft at its low altitude, it was heading straight down into the ocean. It smashed with tremendous impact, killing the crewmember. The rescue helicopter arrived almost instantly on the scene, and the emergency divers retrieved the pilot's sinking body from the deployed parachute.

The accident review board determined that the probable cause of this accident was that only one of the two three hundred-gallon fuel tanks was full. These fuel tanks, carried under each wing, weigh about two thousand pounds apiece. This meant the starboard fuel tank was empty, and the port side tank weighed two thousand pounds more and became an asymmetrical weight that could not be overcome with normal control methods.

During the external pre-flight, the pilot was supposed to remove the fuel cap and visually check that each tank was full. Unfortunately for the pilot, it appeared that he had not made this critical check. Once again, attention to detail raised its ugly head.

With this aviator's death, the count of lost pilots in our squadron on this cruise rose to three, proving that, even in peacetime, carrier aviation is extremely hazardous. This event was to have a contributing effect on my decision later when it came time to either make the navy my career or leave the service to return to civilian life.

On April 7, 1966, two hundred miles off the New York coastline, in a terrible storm that produced heavy spray over the bow of the carrier, the USS Forrestal launched all of its squadron's aircraft to return to their home bases. Our squadron ended its "exchange duty" by flying back to Lemoore Naval Air Station in California and, once again, regained its status as a West Coast Squadron.

Jules at age ten

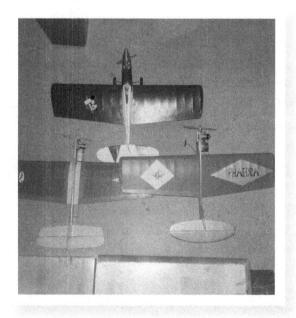

A few of the model airplanes I built

Jules in dress blues, 1964

Sandy and Jules at ball in Pensacola

NAVCAD Harper, 1964

First solo flight, 1964

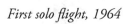

*Getting ready to fly the T-28
at Whiting Field, Florida*

Single-seat AF-9 Cougar Jet, 1965 (US Navy photo)

Gruman F-11A Supersonic tiger Jets
(US Navy photo)

Ensign Harper, 5 aviators over from the left side
of his June 25th graduating class (US Navy photo)

June 26, 1965

*Cutting the cake with
my navy sword*

Trip to California, 1965

Russian Bear flying over USS Forrestal, 1966
(US Navy photo)

Jules at twenty-four-years-old

USS Kitty Hawk (US Navy photo)

VA 112 Broncos, 1966 (US Navy photo)

Jules preparing for mission over North Vietnam, 1967

Broncos preparing for mission.

VA-112 Skyhawk returning to ship after combat mission, 1967 (US Navy photo)

A-4 Skyhawks being refueled by A-3 tanker (US Navy photo)

A-4C normal carrier landing (US Navy photo)

*John Lockard's Skyhawk going into the ship's barricade, 1967
(US Navy photo)*

Battle damage to left wing of Skyhawk on January 21, 1967

F-4 Phantom dropping bombs on ARC Light mission, 1968
(US Navy photo)

A-4 dropping Napalm bomb like we did in Khe Sanh
(US Navy photo)

A-4 Skyhawk after sustaining battle damage by surface-to-air missile (US Navy photo)

Flight deck of USS Kitty Hawk (US Navy photo)

Tonkin Gulf Two Hundred Mission Club

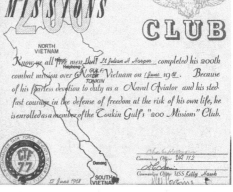

*Continental Airlines Captain Jules Harper
in the cockpit of a Boeing 777*

Veteran's Dedication of the Flagpole Project, November 11, 2014

Jules and Sandy at the Wounded Warriors
of South Florida Gala Ball, 2014

Jules and Sandy at their fiftieth-anniversary party, cutting the
cake using the same sword they used the day they were married

"Bringing the War to the Enemy" presentation, 2015

Jules in the Vietnam section of the Navy Museum in Fort Lauderdale, Florida, with his old flight gear, 2015

★ ★ ★ ★ ★

Part II

THE MAKING
OF A WARRIOR

★ ★ ★ ★ ★

Chapter 5
LEAVING PORT; JUNGLE SURVIVAL

V A-112, the Broncos, enjoyed their short five months at home before all 130 officers and enlisted men deployed in November, 1966, this time to the Western Pacific, (Wes Pac). The times were changing. Many of the naval aviators who had made the Mediterranean cruise were up for normal rotation and left our squadron to go elsewhere.

My "big brother," Phil Sisney, was one of those aviators. Phil had been a distinguished fighter pilot prior to coming over to the Skyhawks and had flown the F-8 Crusader, which was a supersonic jet fighter.

In my short period of time in the squadron, I had gone from being an inexperienced ensign, subjected to tasks like the mail buoy watch, ticker tape duty, and other demeaning jobs, to becoming a fairly experienced naval aviator. As such, I challenged Phil to an air-to-air combat sortie between the two of us. As a former, seasoned fighter pilot, he lightheartedly accepted my invitation, and soon we were in the restricted airspace area designated for conducting those sort of operations.

We hassled each other three different times. Each time, I would wind up at his six o'clock position declaring victory. If that wasn't bad enough for his ego, he also severely pulled some muscles in his neck while turning his head to look for me. This required him to wear a neck brace for several weeks before he left the navy to go to work for Continental Airlines.

The last day he was at the squadron, I thanked him for all the "help" he had given me as my big brother when I was the new guy, or "boot" as rookies are known in the navy. As he was walking out of the squadron, still wearing the neck brace, I reminded him of all the pranks he had played on me and told him, "Pay back is hell." Even with all the jokes and serious events that occurred during each of our lives, Phil and I remained good friends until his death in 2015.

In November, 1966, we cruised out of the Port of San Diego aboard the USS Kitty Hawk CVA-63 that was named after Kitty Hawk, North Carolina. This site was about four miles from where Orville and Wilbur Wright made the first successful powered flight on December 17, 1903.

The Kitty Hawk had a displacement of eighty thousand tons, a length of 1,047, a flight deck width of 252 feet, a draft of thirty-five feet, and could make a speed in excess of thirty knots. It was built by the New York Shipbuilding Corp. in Camden, New Jersey, and was launched on May 21, 1960. It was the second ship to be named Kitty Hawk. The first Kitty Hawk was an aircraft transport that was used in the World War II and played a key role in building up the defenses of Midway and Guadalcanal in 1942.

The "Hawk," as it was affectionately known by its crew, was now the home for about five thousand officers and enlisted men, including our squadron of 130 men. We were made up of twenty-two naval aviators, two maintenance officers, one air intelligence officer, and 105 enlisted men. After stops in Hawaii, Yokosuka, Japan, and Cubi Point, located in Subic Bay, Philippines, we had reached our jumping off point for conducting combat operations in Vietnam.

We had trained all along the way for both nuclear and conventional aerial warfare. Even though we had completed an "escape and evasion" course in the states prior to leaving, we were required to attend another one in Subic Bay. We were given the choice of attending a three- or seven-day survival course, complete with living in the jungle, which was similar to the jungles of Vietnam. This course was mandatory before you could begin combat flying. I wisely elected to take the three-day course.

Our first day was in a classroom, listening to our Filipino instructor/guide named Roberto tell us how to survive in the jungle. There was a stuffed bat with a wing spread of about five feet mounted on the wall above the podium. It was explained to us that it was a vegetarian and would not harm us. It was frightening to see any kind of a bat that big, but it was really frightening to see thousands of them blocking out the sun each afternoon before sunset as we hiked through the jungle!

Roberto had participated in World War II as an enlisted fighter in the Philippine Army. He told us he and his men could smell the Japanese troops before they could see them as they wore cologne. They would try to catch the Japanese fighters as they were exposed, crossing creeks or small rivers. After killing many of them using bows and arrows, he received a field promotion to the rank of captain and continued to kill the "Japs" (I'm using his verbiage).

He was no more than five feet tall and was strong and fast. It turned out the trails through the jungle had a height of about five feet, making it easy for him to move rapidly over the paths. My class was made up of Americans with an average height of about five and one half feet to over six feet tall. Needless to say, we moved more slowly through the jungle.

The first night we were instructed to use bamboo to build our individual sleeping area above the ground so the vipers would not join us in our sleeping bags. We were also told to check our boots in the morning before we put them on to make sure there were no scorpions or other creatures in them.

For dinner that night, Roberto killed a small, furry bat using a sling shot. He roasted the hair off of it over our campfire and asked us if we would like a bite. None of us took him up on his offer! He showed us that everything you can find in a super market is also available in the jungle; you just have to know which plant produced what. The only thing that was not available was salt. For that, you had to go to the ocean.

I did not eat much of anything for my three-day experience, returning to the ship a little thinner. When my squadron mates returned after their seven day "ordeal," as they called it, they agreed, to the man, that their idea to extend for seven days was the dumbest decision they had ever made.

Chapter 6
FIRST COMBAT FLIGHT; CHUCK HILL'S STORY

e arrived on "Yankee Station," a moving position in the Gulf of Tonkin where our aircraft carriers operated, conducting strikes against the enemy, the first part of December, 1966.

My first mission was flown on December 4th in the A-4C aircraft, bureau number 145077, for a total flight time of one hour and forty minutes. My flight of four were sent down to South Vietnam to work with a forward air controller (FAC). The FAC was an air force pilot flying an O-1, single-engine, propeller-driving aircraft. Because of his relatively slow speed, he could find targets that the faster jets could not locate. The FAC also communicated with forces on the ground to help locate them and insure he would not send in strikes against friendly troops.

When he determined where he wanted the bombs, rockets, etc. to land, he would mark the position using smoke grenades or white phosphorus rockets. He would then tell the flight leaders of the jet aircraft how many "klicks" away from the smoke he wanted the weapons to hit. One klick equaled one thousand meters, or one kilometer, and was much faster and easier to say.

Although the FAC was a relatively easy target to hit with sophisticated weapons, the enemy learned that if they shot at a FAC they were going to be bombed by the air force or navy fighter bombers very quickly.

After all the buildup and preparedness to fly strikes against the enemy, this first mission went off without a hitch. I had been very apprehensive—or just down right scared—prior to my launch off the carrier. Once airborne, I settled down to the job of flying the aircraft and executing the mission.

We arrived at the target area the FAC had assigned us and dropped our bombs on a heavily wooded area that was being used as a gathering spot for the Viet Cong. After we had expended all our weapons and were proceeding outbound, the FAC came on the radio and told us we had destroyed several trucks and he could see numerous bodies lying around the bombed site. I had known that people were going to be killed by our aircraft weapons when I was going through training, but to actually participate and see it occur was another thing.

In Yokosuka, Japan, I had purchased a shotgun-type vest that had a lot of holders on it for extra shells. I filled these holders up with Tootsie Rolls, which seemed like a good idea at the time. I thought if I was shot down I would have enough food to get me though a couple of days. Operating in close to one hundred-degree heat, it didn't take long to figure out that the candy was melting and becoming just a sticky mess, so I stopped wearing it.

I assisted a squadron mate of mine, Lt. Chuck Hill, in writing about his first mission over North Vietnam. It was published in the *Bronco Bulletin*, which we sent home to our families. Chuck's flight leader was LCDR Ron Campbell. As you can imagine, we worked as a team throughout our cruise, and all of our naval aviators contributed equally to the war effort. Here is what Chuck wrote:

> I had been briefed and re-briefed prior to leaving the states and en route about combat conditions in North Vietnam. Having flown my first hop earlier in the morning against enemy forces in South Vietnam, the weather cleared up North, and I found myself being briefed for my first mission over North Vietnam.
>
> We were to work with one of our destroyers off the coast of North Vietnam. Besides providing air cover in case the destroyer got into trouble with coastal gun positions, we were assigned the task of searching for a known surface-to-air missile (SAM) site and, if located, destroying it.
>
> Ron briefed the hop: "This hop ought to be no sweat, probably just a coastal familiarization flight. It will give you a good chance to stay off the coast and survey one of the bigger cities in North Vietnam, Vinh. The city and coastline are full of guns, so make sure you stay feet wet (over the water) at all times."
>
> Chuck: We finished the brief, took down the side number of our aircraft, and headed up to the flight deck for the launch. As I climbed into my airplane, I couldn't help but feel a little pride as I noticed the weapons hanging under the wings. I knew I was trained to do this job, and if we found the missile site, I felt sure we could hit it.
>
> After takeoff, I discovered my weapon's system wasn't testing exactly right. I figured, no sweat, probably won't even get close to the beach. I'll just fly Ron's wing and keep my eyes open.
>
> Ron: The ship vectored Chuck and myself into position and told us they were preparing to shell the beach. Knowing that Chuck had a bad system, I planned to stay off the coast and

just spot for the ship. We were in our second turn and heading into the beach when I suspected there might be a SAM coming.

Chuck: I was flying a fairly loose wing on Ron—just fat, dumb, and happy, thinking, *Boy, here's the World War II flying ace.* All of a sudden, Ron started moving his aircraft around a lot. So I thought, YES, jinxing is a good idea. Then the movement became violent, and Ron called, "Look out, here they come." *Here what comes?* I thought to myself.

Ron: Two SAMs came at us, both extremely well aimed, and they appeared to be tracking very good. I could see the tail fires of both missiles from a head-on view as they approached from my right side. I felt I had them beat as they approached the intercept point, but I knew they would be very close, especially to Chuck since he was slightly behind me. I could see the first missile turning with us and arcing over to track on us. Both missiles detonated close enough to us that we could feel the concussions.

Chuck: I turned my airplane upside down and pulled towards the deck to stay with Ron. When I looked out the canopy, I saw the fastest moving telephone pole I had ever seen in my life. About as fast as I saw it, it went by.

Then the second one was staring me in the face. I decided it was just about time to get the heck out of there and pulled even harder for the water. I cleared that one, but by this time, I was so scared my knees were like jelly. I couldn't even kick the rudder pedals my legs were shaking so badly.

About that time Ron called and said, "Watch out for the river mouth, or they will hose you down with Triple-A."

Ron: I asked Chuck if he was ok, and he answered that he was. We turned back into the beach to try and get the SAM site, but we couldn't see it. We continued to work with the destroyer below us and finally left for home.

Chuck: When I stepped out of the plane, after making my arrested landing, I took a deep breath—something that for a few brief moments I was sure I would never do again.

Chapter 7
CHARTS OF VIETNAM; WEAPONS OUR SKYHAWKS CARRIED

I n 1965, the air force and navy acknowledged they were having trouble identifying geographical areas in North Vietnam that their surveillance flights were indicating as locations of prime targets. These "prime targets" might be trucks, tanks, railroad cars, troops, or any other moving targets.

To help solve this problem, in December of 1965, air force and navy officials both met and divided North Vietnam into six route package areas, which were easily identifiable. The area starting just above the DMZ was designated Route Package One, and they would work up numerically to Route Package Six, which was the Hanoi and Haiphong areas located in the northern part of Vietnam. Route Package Six was subdivided into Six-A, which was the Hanoi area, and Six-B, which was the Haiphong area. The entire Route Package Six area was considered the most dangerous airspace in the world, due to all the anti-aircraft guns, missiles, and enemy jet fighters.

The navy was assigned the responsibility for Route Packages Two through Four, and Six-B (Haiphong). This was because these areas were adjacent to the Gulf of Tonkin, and we did not have to fly over enemy country to get to the coastal targets. There were times that both the navy and air force worked together to bomb the same route package areas, especially Hanoi.

The navy maintained total air superiority over the Gulf of Tonkin. By combining all the radars from the aircraft, ships, and ground stations, the navy was able to identify threatening aircraft targets that might be heading out into the Gulf. This was especially true in the northern part of the Gulf, where our sea, air, rescue (North SAR) destroyer was on station, working with a pair of jet fighters stationed over its location.

In 1965, a pair of North Vietnamese aircraft left the coastline near Haiphong, heading out into the Gulf where all our ships were located. They were picked up on radar early and a pair of our F-4 Phantom Jets were vectored into a firing position using their sparrow missiles, which can be fired from a head-on position. Both of the hostile enemy aircraft were shot down, and we did not experience any aircraft flying into the Gulf area until 1967, with the same results. After that, no other enemy aircraft ever ventured out into the Gulf during the time I was there.

As good as this was for the navy, the air force had exactly the opposite problem when they flew into the Hanoi area. The North Vietnamese had a very good radar system, and they could see our air force flights coming a long way before they got close to their city. They would vector their jets into our oncoming fighters, which led to many "dog fights" (air-to-air hassling) as it was called.

The A-4C attack aircraft had a pair of 20mm machine guns located close to the fuselage on the wing roots. These machine guns had a "whip barrel" effect when fired, meaning if you were shooting at the ground, the bullets would be spread out in a circular pattern, which was desirable. In a fighter jet, the machine guns shoot straight ahead so you can rely on your aim to hit another airplane. We originally carried two hundred rounds of 20mm ammunition, but that was changed to eighty rounds due to the needed space for the installation of an electronic device known as the ALQ-51, which will be discussed later.

The bombs we carried were, as follows: Mark 81: 250 lbs.; Mark 82: 500 lbs.; Mark 83: 1,000 lbs.; Mark 84: 2,000 lbs.; Mark 117: 750 lbs.; Mark 118: 3,000 lbs.; and cluster bomb units (CBU-24 series bombs).

The missiles we used were, as follows: AGM 45 Shrike, which had a 2.5-pound warhead and was used to temporarily damage SAM missile site radars so the strike force could get in and out safely; 2.75- and 5-inch Zuni rockets that were used against troops, trucks, trains, and the MK 24 flares, which provided light at night.

We also had the AGM 12B and C; this was a Bullpup missile that had a one thousand-pound warhead on it and was guided to the target by the pilot using his left hand while he flew the aircraft with his right hand. He used a small steering stick mounted on the console of the left side of the cockpit to accomplish this. He steered the Bullpup by keeping the flare, installed in the tail of the missile, in sight. By combining the speed of the missile, which was Mach 1.8, and its large warhead, it had tremendous destructive power against whatever targets you were trying to eliminate. This weapon system was like a video game and a lot of fun to use!

In addition, we used 20mm Gatlin guns; this weapon system fired four thousand rounds of 20mm bullets per minute, and the A-4C could carry two on them, one under each wing. As a rule, we could only fill them with a half of a load of ammunition because if the gun "jammed," we would be too heavy to land back aboard the carrier due to the weight of the ammunition.

The bombs were carried under the wings of our aircraft, using either a MER or TER Ejector Rack system. The MER could carry six bombs (two hundred and fifty-pound up to one thousand-pound bombs). The TER rack could carry three, one thousand-pound bombs. The pilot could elect to drop all the bombs at one time or drop any number he wanted to by using a selector switch located on the front instrument panel.

Chapter 8
DANANG; SINGER SEWING MACHINE COMPANY; BULLPUP MISSILE

On December 5, 1966, I was flying my second flight against North Vietnam with a load of MK 81 bombs. Our target was a bridge just south of the Than Hoa area. I rolled into my forty-five-degree dive and tried to release my bombs at an altitude of about five thousand feet.

We had been instructed to never fly below three thousand feet as the trained military gunners and even the farmers could shoot you down if you were that low. We had learned this in the Korean War, with many airplanes lost before we realized the problem.

My bombs would not release, and I struggled to pull my "heavy" jet back up to a higher altitude so I wouldn't be shot down. After going feet wet and going through all the procedures to release the bombs out at sea, the decision was made to send me to Danang as you cannot bring bombs back aboard the aircraft carrier.

I left my flight and proceeded down to South Vietnam alone, over the open ocean. My primary navigation instrument, known as the tacan, was not working. My radio and transponder were in good shape as I talked to the air force controller located in Danang. He gave me vectors, which guided me in the direction of Danang.

As I arrived in the Danang area, it was overcast and raining. I continued to take the controller's vectors and got lined up with the runway. I came down the glideslope through the clouds, following the controller's instructions, landed, and taxied over to the area assigned to me by the ground controller.

I have to say I was very nervous being on the ground in Vietnam. It took about two hours, which seemed like forever, for the ordnance men to unload my bombs, and I was on my way again, thank goodness!

Taxiing out, I was having trouble talking to ground control. As I reached the end of the active taxiway and approached the runway, I switched over to the tower frequency. I called the tower several times and still no joy (could not reach them). It was cloudy, and light rain was still falling, restricting my visibility. After looking both ways on the runway, I made the decision to go ahead and take off because I was scared to be on the ground in Danang. By all standards, this was an unprofessional thing to do.

I took off and climbed out through the clouds, without talking to any controllers. I used a JN chart I carried, which was a map that covers a huge area using a very small chart with little detail. I just eyeballed what I thought was a good heading back out to the ship, several hundred miles away.

My tacan was still not working, so I just flew a heading for a certain amount of time, hoping that I could get close to the ship. As I reached the area I thought to be in close proximity to the ship, I keyed my microphone and said, "Pawtucket strike, this is Montana 401. I estimate I am on your 182-degree radial at approximately thirty-two miles. Over."

Pawtucket (the call sign for the Kitty Hawk) answered and said, "Montana 401, please squawk code 7056 and ident."

I did as I was instructed, and Pawtucket came back and said, "Montana 401, I have you on the 168-degree radial at 41 miles."

I answered him and thought that was pretty darn good to be within twenty miles of the position I thought I had navigated to. I made a normal landing, if there is such a thing on the carrier, and was glad to be back aboard the ship. Thanks to flying solo in a single-seat jet and being in a war-time environment, I never said or heard a thing about my actions leaving Danang.

There are only four reasons I lived through my experiences in Vietnam. They were the training I received from the US Navy, luck, prayers, and the Singer Sewing Machine Company.

The Singer Sewing Machine Company had a division that specialized in electronic counter measures. Specifically, they built a device known as the ALQ-51. Simply stated, this piece of gear took in the radar signal that was interrogating your aircraft and sent it back to the radar operator slightly altered. The signal it sent back showed that you were two hundred feet behind where you actually were. When the enemy radar was operating in the automatic mode, it issued control signals to either the SAM missile or anti-aircraft batteries that were aiming at your aircraft. It caused either one of these devices to miss the target and was very effective.

Unfortunately, Vietnam had Russian "technicians" who came along with the SAM missiles they were supplying, with the intent to shoot our aircraft down. A good technician could read through the altered signals he was looking at and manually instruct the missile to move forward two hundred feet and hit the target. This is one of the reasons we lost many airplanes to the SAM missiles.

The ALQ-51 also gave the pilot audio warnings when a missile was fired, and the audio portion then switched to a high pulse rate frequency

(PRF) when the missile was actually tracking your aircraft. This allowed the pilot to go into a mode of "jinxing" (moving the aircraft up, down, left, right) in a violent manner to make the jet a harder target to hit.

It also gave the pilot time to punch a button that sent a signal to shotgun-type shells located in the tail of the aircraft, thereby releasing a material known as "chaff." Chaff is material that resembles aluminum foil and was designed to confuse the radar operator by sending back signals that were, at the least, cluttered. The hope was to keep the operator from hitting your aircraft with the weapon system he was controlling.

Another thing that helped pilots avoid being hit by ground fire was the humidity in Vietnam. Vietnam was very humid most of the time. When anti-aircraft guns were shooting at your airplane, you could actually look out the cockpit canopy and see the bullets coming up at you as they were leaving a trail behind them. This was caused by the bullets moving at a fast speed through the humid air. A good analogy of this is when an airliner is flying through humid air during takeoff or landing. By looking out of the windows, the passengers can see the parting of the air stream as it passes over and off the wings.

To understand the effects of humidly even further, consider one of my later flights. We were attacking gun positions located on an island close to Haiphong. I was flying the fourth position in the division. My plane was carrying 2.75 rockets, which were very effective against troops and anti-aircraft cannons.

The air was humid as usual, and as I rolled in on the target, I found myself right in the middle of a quad-mounted, liquid-cooled, 23mm, radar-controlled, anti-aircraft cannon. Each of the barrels had a thousand-round-per-minute rate of fire, which meant that the weapon system could put up four thousand rounds per minute. This was another weapon system the Russians were supplying North Vietnam to use against our aircraft, and it was very effective at destroying many of our planes.

I could see a steady line of bullets passing over, under, left of, and right of my A-4. I was right in the middle of all these bullets, and I thought to myself, *It's going to be impossible to pull out of this dive without getting hit.* I fired my rockets and began a hard, six g pull back up to level flight. I continued the pull to a forty-five-degree angle climb right up into an overcast weather situation. Miraculously, none of the bullets hit my aircraft during the attack. My scan went from outside the canopy back inside the cockpit to check the attitude indicator. It was solid overcast, and I corrected the aircraft attitude using the gyro like we had done in training to regain normal flight operation.

During the debrief, I learned that none of the three other pilots saw any hostile fire at all. Unfortunately, this happened many times to other flights. One jet would get shot down, but no one else saw anything!

On December 10, 1966, I was assigned a target that was located on Route One, just south of Vinh, North Vietnam. Route One connects the northern part of North Vietnam to South Vietnam. It was a major supply route for trucks delivering weapons and supplies to their troops in the South.

The weather that day was very clear, and I found the target with no problem. It was a concrete bridge that had been bombed previously but had been repaired to keep it operational. As was mentioned earlier, the Bullpup or AGM 12B, had a one thousand-pound warhead. The missile accelerates to almost twice the speed of sound, 1.8 Mach, hitting its target with an explosive force much greater than a normal MK 83 one thousand-pound bomb.

I put the Skyhawk in a shallow dive several miles away from the target and released the Bullpup missile from an altitude of about five thousand feet. Steering was easy by using the control stick with my left hand. The flare, located in the tail of the Bullpup, was very visible, enabling me to guide the missile to a direct hit on the bridge.

Not only was the bridge hit, it was totally destroyed! There was nothing left where it had been but a missing gap between each end of the highway.

On a later mission involving the Bullpup missiles, I was on an Alpha strike (large strike sometimes including multi-carrier attacks on the same target) and was given the task of flak suppression.

Our target was in Route Package Six-B, the Haiphong area. The large anti-aircraft gun position was easy to spot at a distance of about ten miles. The weather was clear, and the guns were set up in a circular pattern. As our strike group approached, the gunners began to fire at us. I can still remember vividly each of the guns firing in turn, one right after another, working their way around the circular gun battery position.

The Bullpup missiles can be fused to detonate when they strike the ground for a hardened target like the bridge, or they can be fused to go off above ground to affect a larger, populated area. In this case, they were fused to go off above ground.

I fired the first of my two Bullpup missiles at the 100mm anti-aircraft weapon system. After the Bullpup hit the target, I fired the second missile at the same target. As it was being steered to the target, I noticed one or two guns would fire and the next one or two would not fire. Obviously, my first Bullpup missile had done its job well! After the second missile hit, the entire anti-aircraft battery stopped firing.

I then reversed my course and went back out to a feet-wet position. I couldn't help but think, *Give me the biggest weapon I can carry and provide me with the maximum stand-off distance.* This would be the best possible system to have as an attack pilot. My thinking was pretty good as proven by drone strike use in later wars.

Chapter 9
BOMBING THE VINH AIRFIELD;
JUNIOR OFFICERS' BUNKROOM

The City of Vinh is located close to the coastline of North Vietnam and was the closest airfield to our carrier's normal Yankee Station position. If a Mig fighter had taken off from Vinh, it would have been a quick flight to our ship's position. For that reason, the navy was tasked with the responsibility of keeping the runway damaged so it was unusable for their fighters.

On January 18, 1967, our ship ran an Alpha strike against the Vinh Airfield. My division of A-4s (a flight of four) were each loaded with two MK 84 bombs to be used against the airfield. These bombs were two thousand pounds and filled with highly explosive material. The fuses were set to detonate the bombs slightly less than one second after they hit the ground. This gave the bombs time to penetrate the runway, and when they exploded, they would create large craters. Our flight was briefed to drop the bombs on different sections of the field so the entire runway would be damaged.

Besides our division of A-4s, our sister squadron, VA-144, the "Road Runners," sent a division of A-4s that were armed with five-inch Zuni rockets that were to be used to knock out the anti-aircraft weapon systems defending the field. VA-75, the "Sunday Punchers," were sending four A-6s armed with twenty-eight MK 82 bombs (five hundred pounds each). The A-6 had two engines and could carry more bombs than any other plane we had on the carrier. Not only could it carry all these weapons, it could out run the F-4 Phantoms over a long distance when the Phantoms were fully loaded with bombs.

Shortly after taking off from the carrier, we assembled our strike force, with our F-4 Phantoms used as fighter protection against Migs, and proceeded into the coastline near Vinh. Our position in the flight was scheduled to arrive at the target last. We were following the flight of four A-6s by about two miles. During my training to be a naval aviator, I was assured that if I ever got hit so bad that I was going to crash, I could always eject and come floating down to earth safely by using a parachute. As we approached the shore line, one of the A-6s ahead of us got hit and cut in half by a large anti-aircraft cannon projectile. The twenty-eight, five hundred-pound bombs on board the aircraft exploded along with the jet fuel, making two huge, distinct fire balls that drifted very slowly down towards earth.

After several seconds, both the pilot and the bombardier-navigator (BN) ejected. I thought to myself, *Thank God they both made it out.* The ejection seat rocket carried the seat and the occupants up and away from the fire balls that were still drifting slowly towards the ground. Both parachutes appeared to open normally, and the two crew members began to float down to the ground. But what happened next was horrific. The crew members and their parachutes were descending faster than the fireballs, and very quickly, they were all engulfed in flames. The burning pilot and bombardier-navigator were now attached to streaming parachutes that were on fire, providing no protection at all. Next, they slammed into the ground at a very high rate of speed, insuring their deaths. It was mercifully fast, but that is a sight I will never forget. And, so much for floating to the ground safely.

Living on an aircraft carrier, with a population of about five thousand men, was a unique experience in itself. I was one of five naval aviators and one air intelligence officer sharing our squadron's junior officers' bunkroom on-board the ship. Each of us had our own bunk bed, desk, a few drawers, and closet.

Two of our naval aviators, Jerry Hogan and Alexander (Doc) Palenscar, were Naval Academy graduates. The other three aviators, including myself, had come into naval aviation by completing the NAVCAD program, which only required two years of college. Our air intelligence officer, Jim Gibson, was a college graduate.

As we passed through Hawaii, we purchased enough floor carpet to make "wall-to-wall" coverage possible for our bunkroom. With two members playing the guitar and other members of the room learning to play, thanks to instruction given by Tom Baggett, plus all the other noise that is made by six men, noise suppression was desperately needed! Lucky for us, the carpet did lower the noise to an acceptable level.

The "head" (bathroom) was located a short fifty yards from the bunkroom. Normally we had plenty of fresh water, but occasionally we were forced to use salt water for our showers. This occurred when several of the evaporators, used to convert salt water into fresh water, were inoperative. The steam catapult system used to launch aircraft from the flight deck also relied on the use of fresh water, and it took priority over showers.

Our short stay in Yokosuka, Japan, gave all of us a chance to purchase almost every known stereo component that was available at the time. You can imagine the time it took to get it all hooked up in our junior officers' bunkroom. Once that was done, many more hours were spent copying music from each other's collections.

Our bunkroom, because of its size, was the gathering place for other officers who wanted to get together to talk and socialize. We even had the XO (executive officer) of the Kitty Hawk, Thomas Hudner, in the room one evening for a big get together. Captain Hudner told us an amazing story about how he had been awarded the Congressional Medal of Honor for his flying actions in the Korean conflict. More on that subject in another chapter.

During many of our bunkroom conversations, we thoroughly discussed most of the aspects of the war. Our unified position on the war in Vietnam came down to the following: "It's a nasty war, but it's the only war we have." We all carried out our missions in a truly professional manner, bringing the war to the enemy. Politically at that point in our lives, we were all right of Attila the Hun!

By the time we started flying missions over Vietnam, participating in Operation Rolling Thunder (March 2, 1965–November 2, 1968), we had formed good friendships with each other. Three of us, Jerry Hogan, Doc Palenscar, and myself were especially close and had grown mustaches, which were quite a sight to see.

Chapter 10

FIRST COMBAT LOSS; BARRICADE; THE PREMONITION

Fighting a war is a 24/7 operation. The carriers on Yankee Station divided up the responsibility of day and night (called red carrier) operations. Red carrier began at midnight and ceased at noon the same day when the other carrier picked up the operations.

Our ship was on the red carrier cycle during January, 1967. It was normal for all of us to fly at least one flight a day. LTJG Jerry Hogan was the first pilot of our bunkroom to launch that night at midnight on the 21st of January, which would turn out to be a devastating day for our squadron.

Jerry was an extremely friendly and wonderful person. He was the type of individual that as soon as you met him, you knew you had made another best friend. He was a very good pilot, like all of us in the squadron. Everyone respected and admired him.

His flight had been briefed to conduct an armed reconnaissance mission over the Song Yen River, located just a few miles south of Thanh Hoa. Thanh Hoa was a good-sized coastal city and was heavily defended. They were to drop flares from their aircraft, looking for trucks, barges, etc. Jerry's aircraft assignment that day was Montana 415, bureau number 145144. All of our squadron pilots flew different aircraft on any given day. I had flown Jerry's aircraft, Montana 415, about a month before on December 20, 1966.

After Jerry launched from the carrier, he rendezvoused with the rest of his flight, and they headed for the coastline of North Vietnam. Flares were dropped over a ferry landing, and Jerry noted several barges. He called "rolling in," which was a standard call we all made in that type of flight. His bombs were seen exploding, followed by another huge explosion, which his wingman thought was his aircraft hitting the ground.

Jerry was carried Missing in Action (MIA) for years and was promoted to the rank of lieutenant commander. He was born on February 28, 1940, in Tuscaloosa, Alabama. Neither his body nor his remains were ever found. He is honored on panel 14E, row 63 of the Vietnam Wall that was built in 1982 to honor Vietnam Veterans and "heal the wounds of a nation." A marker in his memory is also placed at Arlington National Cemetery.

Ensign John Lockard was a tall, slim, slow-talking officer who was also well respected by our entire squadron. He was the second member of our bunkroom to fly that morning as part of a three-carrier strike mission that began on January 20th and continued through the 21st. This type of multi-carrier strike was known as an Alpha strike. It consisted of each carrier attacking the target, followed by the next carrier's aircraft attacking the same target area against the rail and bridge complexes at Ninh Binh. Ninh Binh is located about twenty nautical miles north of Thanh Hoa and fifty nautical miles south of Hanoi.

The following is part of a press release article that I helped to write about one of our pilots that was published in *Naval Aviation News* for the mission that occurred on January 21, 1967:

When they completed their strikes against the Dong Phong Thuong military storage and transshipment complex in North Vietnam, navy pilots wrapped up what was then the biggest carrier-based assault of 1967 on enemy supply routes. Considered by navy sources to be one of four major "hubs" in the relay of war supplies to South Vietnam, the complex was considered very important.

Rear Admiral David C. Richardson, commander of Task Force 77 operating off Vietnam on board the USS Kitty Hawk, said Dong Phong Thuong was a marshalling point for southbound supplies carried by road and rail from Hanoi and by barges from Haiphong. It was also a major stockpile area for communist war material.

To knock out the complex, aircraft were launched on two-day co-coordinated strike missions from the Seventh Fleet carriers: USS Kitty Hawk, USS Coral Sea, and USS Ticonderoga. F-4 Phantoms, F-8 Crusaders, A-4 Skyhawks, and A-6 Intruders battered the target area.

Primary objectives included two rail bridges and a two hundred-foot pontoon bridge spanning the nearby Song Lau River, a ferry, five warehouses, four cave storage areas and supply routes. But there were also other targets. The missions, some of them described by returning pilots, went like this:

Skyhawks from VA-112 streaked in on a cable bridge and inflicted heavy damage with 500-pound bombs. "We hit the southern end of the bridge," LTJG Karl Jadrnicek said later. "I was the last in on the target, and I had a bird's-eye view of our bombs going off as they hit the bridge. I looked back on the area after I pulled out and could see it burning on the southern abutment."

Bomb assessment photography taken by reconnaissance pilots after the strikes showed that all three bridges were knocked out and the ferry sunk. Two warehouses were completely destroyed, and three were heavily damaged. As a bonus, a number of boxcars from three trains—trapped on a spur by previous strikes—were destroyed or derailed. After the missions were over, rail lines were reported out in six places, including the entrance and exit to the transshipment complex. Besides silencing many AA batteries protecting the complex, the pilots also knocked out several surface-to-air missile (SAM) facilities.

Ensign John Lockard was assigned to fly on the skipper's wing, number two position, in a flight of four Skyhawks to take part in the attack bombing bridges mentioned above. He was carrying six MK 82 (five hundred-pound bombs). Rolling into his dive, following the flak suppressor element, everything went normally until he pulled up out of the dive. As he was regaining altitude, he was hit in the left fuselage tail section with what was believed to be a 37mm anti-aircraft cannon. With his fire warning light on, a loss of hydraulic pressure, and tail hook damaged, he was able to make it back out to sea.

While going back to the carrier, he extinguished the fire in the fuselage and waited until all the other returning aircraft had been recovered before he came in for his carrier landing. There was a lot of concern that his tail hook was damaged to the extent that it might not hold the aircraft when it landed. The decision was made by the captain and air boss of the Kitty Hawk to bring him in for a "barricade" landing.

The barricade was specifically designed to stop aircraft on the flight deck when their tail hook was thought to be inoperative. John made a normal landing, and his plane ran into the barricade. It looked like a large, net-type device stretched across the flight deck, similar to a tennis net. It was the first barricade landing ever made on the Kitty Hawk, and, fortunately, John was not injured. For his superb airmanship, Ensign Lockard was awarded the **Distinguished Flying Cross**.

Most of our squadron not working on the flight deck came into our ready room to watch Ensign Lockard land his Skyhawk into the barricade. This was being filmed by the "PLAT." PLAT is an acronym for pilot's landing aid television. The camera was buried in the flight deck and filmed each aircraft as it landed aboard the carrier. There were other cameras located on the carrier's island, which could be directed towards whatever object you wanted to film, and those films were shown in all the ready rooms throughout the ship.

The landing signaling officer (LSO) used the PLAT to debrief the flight crews after each of their "passes" (landing segment of their flight on the aircraft carrier). It was very important that the pilots flew the prescribed glide slope, which was seven hundred fpm descent, to land on the carrier. If you were too "shallow" by one or two degrees, you ran the risk of landing long and being in a bolter situation. If your angle was too steep, like four or five degrees, you would hit too hard and possibly damage the aircraft's landing gear or, worse yet, hit the round down. The round down was the stern or back end of the flight deck, and as the name implies, it was rounded in case a plane hit it during landing.

No matter how many times you have landed on an aircraft carrier, each pass is graded by the LSO, who is also a naval aviator. He keeps a record of all your "passes" in a logbook so he can determine if you are developing any bad habits during the landing portion of your flight.

The LSO debriefed each pilot who landed during that particular cycle. Being debriefed by the LSO can be very interesting as he must explain to you what happened on your last pass and how you should correct any deficiencies. As you can imagine, some of the pilots may not agree with the LSO's version of what he saw, and many stimulating conversations occurred—with the LSO almost always winning!

Later in the day, I found myself briefing my twenty-sixth mission with LCDR Jim Lucchesi. We were on the last flight launch of red carrier, which departed at about half past nine in the morning, and we were going to return to the Dong Phong Thuong area. Our assigned task for this mission was being flak suppressers, using sixteen, five-inch Zuni rockets to knock out enemy gun positions.

The Zuni rockets were loaded four to a container, and we carried four containers on our aircraft, two under each wing. We could fire two containers at a time or all four at one time, which we elected to do on this mission. We would only be making one run on this target as it was heavily defended. If you made more than one run, after the first one, the gunners on the ground had a better chance of shooting you down as they knew the direction you were coming in from.

We briefed to operate as a "section" (two aircraft) while attacking our target. A section flight is very maneuverable and can attack from a different direction than the rest of the strike group. We finished our briefing, and as we were getting ready to go "topside" (upstairs), I had a premonition that I was going to be "hit" during this mission. Out of all the missions I flew over Vietnam, this was the only one where I ever had this sort of premonition.

I remember sitting in the A-4, waiting my turn for the cat shot. I became so nervous that after I was launched off the flight deck, I had to loosely hold the stick to keep from shaking the aircraft. I rendezvoused with my section leader, Jim Lucchesi, and we joined up with the rest of the strike group as we proceeded into the target area.

It was a very clear day for Vietnam, and the visibility was greater than twenty miles. I began to relax when, suddenly, the big guns started shooting at our group from the ground, completely overcasting the sky above us with flak in a matter of minutes. No longer nervous or scared,

I visually acquired my target and rolled in, firing my Zuni rockets at the enemy position. A hail of bullets was passing my aircraft, but luck was with me; they all missed.

As my wingman, Jim Lucchesi, and I were leaving the target area, we proceeded in a southerly direction and soon found ourselves under attack by radar-controlled guns. We were increasing our speed to over four hundred knots when I looked over towards Jim's airplane and noticed he was being tracked with flak, which was exploding about two hundred feet behind him.

I called for a "break" (change in the aircraft's altitude and heading) and explained to Jim what I saw behind his aircraft. We steadied up on a new heading and altitude when, after about thirty seconds, the gun fire began to track Jim's aircraft again. I called another break, and we climbed back up to a higher altitude and different heading. We had just steadied up on this new course when I felt a large concussion in my ears. Jim's aircraft began to leave me behind, and I checked my engine instruments to make sure the engine was working properly. I had lost one hundred knots of airspeed. The engine RPM gauge showed that it was putting out 102 rpms, exactly what it should have been doing at wide open throttle, which is what I was asking for.

I looked out towards my right wing and checked it, or checked as much as I could see. It appeared to be fine. As my head started to move around towards the left side of the aircraft, I got that feeling in my stomach that we all have occasionally when we know something is wrong.

When I saw the left wing, it became apparent what the problem was. The last three to six feet of the wing was gone. I was looking at jagged metal running in a diagonal direction from the front of the wingtip to a position that ran off the wing and continued in a direction that took off half of the aircraft's port aileron. It appeared, and was later confirmed by maintenance, that the anti-aircraft projectile that hit my wing did not explode. If it had, the aircraft and I would have been destroyed!

I was still deep in enemy country, about ten minutes away from feet wet, and my aircraft would only make a speed of about three hundred knots. I knew I had to make a distress call and let Jim know what had happened to me.

We were living in a time I call the John Wayne era. No matter how bad you were hit, you had to be "cool." I prepared the statement I was going to send out on the radio in a very calm, cool voice and keyed the radio mike button. Then I screamed, "Help, I've been hit!" Instead of a deep, commanding voice, my transmission came out in a high, squeaky tone that was several octaves higher than I had hoped for. So much for being the John Wayne type.

I made it to feet wet, and Jim joined up with me. We climbed to ten thousand feet to conduct a slow flight test of the airplane. This was necessary to see if it would continue to fly at the slow approach speed needed to land on the carrier. If it would not fly slowly enough, due to the missing part of the wing, I would set up to eject in a controlled environment, which would be close to the ship with the ship's plane guard helicopter waiting to pick me up after I parachuted into the water. Fortunately, the plane handled well enough for me to get back aboard the carrier. As I taxied out of the arresting gear, the air boss transmitted a call over the radio to me saying, "Looks like termites, Montana" (our official navy call sign). I acknowledged his transmission and parked my aircraft. Premonition confirmed!

At the end of that day, my confidence in making it through the cruise alive was not very high. Three of the five aviators in our bunkroom had been hit, one of them fatally. I sent my wife, Sandy, a telegram explaining what was happening over in the combat zone. I asked her to take a leave from teaching school on the base and fly over and meet me at our next in-port period. She checked with her school principal, and he agreed to let her go for a couple of weeks. It turned out that another squadron mate, Mike Gump, already had plans to have his wife join him during the in-port period. We were good friends, and we both agreed to take some of our military leave. The four of us toured the Philippines and Hong Kong together.

Our line period on Yankee Station was over on February 15, 1967. Instead of staying on-board the ship, with our skipper's approval, Mike and I flew our Skyhawks to Cubi Point, the naval station located in Subic Bay, Philippines. This gave us several more days of leave to enjoy with our wives. The two of us arranged travel to Manila, where we met our wives, took a tour of the city, and then flew in an old DC-3 up to Baguio, located on the island of Luzon. We checked into Camp John Hay that was being run by the US Air Force as a rest and relaxation resort.

The elevation there was about five thousand feet, making it much cooler than Manila. We played golf one day on the John Hay golf course and enjoyed trying our skills on cardiac hill. That golf hole was divided into three tiers, with the green being above the third tier. The incline was so severe that they actually had a rope tow, similar to the type used at the ski areas, located on one side of the fairway to help pull you up the steep grade.

After a few days of relaxing at camp John Hay, we flew to Hong Kong, checked into the Peninsula Hotel, and met our carrier. Our squadron got an "admin ashore," a hotel room where we could meet and leave our shopping items instead of returning to the ship. We enjoyed seeing some of the Asian sights during the day, including a tour from which we could see Communist China in the distance. In the evenings, we had several parties with our squadron mates in the admin hotel room. Visiting with my wife ended too quickly, and on March 3, 1967, I was flying combat missions once again.

Chapter 11
TET; NANCY SINATRA; THE VIGILANTE

et is the Vietnamese New Year. It usually occurs in January or
February and is a time for the Vietnamese people to celebrate.
Many families get together and cook large meals, forgetting their
troubles of the past year and hoping for a better one to come.

President Johnson ordered a "cease fire" from February 8th through
February 12th, 1967, to honor this holiday. On the night of February
7th, four of our pilots flying their Skyhawks were assigned to go into
North Vietnam, west of Thanh Hoa, and bomb a truck park. A truck park
was an area where the Vietnamese parked their trucks, usually under the
canopy of trees, to hide from the view of our airplanes. Reconnaissance
photos for that day had shown numerous trucks hidden in this park.

Our pilots had launched on the last cycle of the night, between ten
and eleven o'clock. They located the target and dropped their bombs
on the trucks about 11:50 p.m. On their way back to feet wet, they

passed over Route One, which was the major highway between North and South Vietnam. It was a clear night, and they said they could see the lights from Hanoi about forty miles to the north. Tet and the cease fire were to begin at midnight, which was in five minutes.

As I recall, the flight leader told me that suddenly hundreds of vehicle lights lit up the highway. The trucks, cars, and anything else that could move were heading south to take advantage of the Tet cease fire. Apparently, they did not have their clocks synchronized to the correct time and started their movement a few minutes early.

To me this seemed like a tremendous violation of the spirit of President Johnson's cease fire. I remembered this vividly a year later when Tet was to begin on January 31, 1968. We briefed a night trip to go into Vietnam, just north of Vinh, less than an hour before Tet was to start. It was the same time frame as the flight the previous year where the pilots had observed all the vehicles moving south just minutes before the official start of Tet. Our flight of four was to do a road reconnaissance mission, which meant we were looking for any moving vehicles and destroying them. We discussed what had happened the year before and were determined to take advantage of their clocks being a little fast.

When we reached the beach as we called it, there were no lights on any highway we could see. We flew well inland, and as the clock approached midnight, we were positioned over Route One, waiting for the trucks to turn on their lights and begin the movement of supplies south. Just as the previous year, five minutes early, the Vietnamese drivers turned on their lights. We could not believe the number of vehicles involved in this operation. There was a solid line of lights as far as we could see to the north and to the south.

We had divided our division into two sections, spread out from one another to cover more territory, and began to bomb the vehicles on the highway. As you can imagine, we flew over Vietnam with our running lights turned off so the gunners could not see us. The night darkness hid us well until we released our bombs. There was a shotgun-type shell that kicked off each bomb, and it made quite a flash in doing so. The gunners on the ground knew what to look for and, seeing the flashes, opened up on us as we began to pull out from our bomb runs. The tracers from their anti-aircraft weapons looked like garden hoses turned on with the water flowing out, spraying from side to side.

Our four-plane division destroyed many trucks, cars, and other moving vehicles that night. Unfortunately, there were so many vehicles moving that it was just a small dent in their numbers. It was reported later in the war that the North Vietnamese had moved over twenty-five thousand tons of ammunition and other munitions south during this brief pause called Tet!

I was returning to the Hawk after one of my missions in February, 1967, when I received a different sort of radio call prior to landing aboard the carrier. The *Fort Myers News Press* printed the following story:

Hello there! USS Kitty Hawk-LTJG Jules Harper was preparing his A4C Skyhawk for a landing aboard this carrier when a smooth, feminine voice came over the airwaves.

"You're cleared to land downwind," whispered The Voice. Harper thought for a moment he was losing his grip, but he went ahead and landed anyway. His first request was to meet The Voice. As it turned out, The Voice also had a body, belonging to Nancy Sinatra, who was aboard the carrier to see if she could make it rock and roll while off Vietnam.

The five thousand officers and men each offered to give the singer a personal tour of the ship. While visiting the ship's primary flight control tower, she was handed the microphone and asked to radio landing clearance to Harper.

The RA-5C Vigilante was a beautiful aircraft, and it was the largest and fastest aircraft to ever operate off of an aircraft carrier. It could reach a speed of Mach 2.5—faster than the smaller jet fighters! The navy had wanted another nuclear-armed aircraft to complement its fleet of manned bombers in the 1950s and came up with the Vigilante. It flew its first flight in Columbus, Ohio, on August 31, 1958. The Vigilante had a lot of developmental problems as it was on the leading edge of technology. Most of these problems were eventually overcome, and the plane had a good service record.

The Vigilante was powered by a pair of J-79 jet engines that were the same engines the F-4 Phantom used. They were separated in the fuselage by a linear bomb bay for the MK 28 nuclear device, the weapon that was normally employed. It was rumored that in early flight testing, when they were trying to simulate dropping a nuclear weapon, the bomb would not eject out of the aircraft. It turned out that severe buffing caused by air circulating between the jet engines at the rear of the aircraft was the reason. Perhaps that was why it ended up being used as a reconnaissance aircraft instead.

Unfortunately, it had the highest loss rate of any navy aircraft used in the Vietnam War, but it was not due to the aircraft. The aircraft was good. But, sometimes it was too fast, and it was being used for flying reconnaissance missions. The speed of the Vigilante was so great that on one run over Hanoi, an accompanying F-4 Phantom pilot said that at full power on both his engines, he was only able to keep up with the Vigilante because his aircraft was on the inside of the turn, making the distance his jet traveled less. As for reconnaissance after an attack, once all the strike group aircraft left the enemy area, the Vigilante had to wait at least ten minutes for all the smoke to clear before it could fly in over the target and take pictures. That delay would give the enemy plenty of time to reload, launch SAMS, and fire anti-aircraft weapons with a technique called "barrage-sector fire."

The Vigilante was hit a lot more than other aircraft because it flew so fast through barrage-sector fire. Barrage-sector fire occurred when the North Vietnamese radar operators saw our aircraft approaching their area. They communicated with the military commander in that region, and he issued orders for everyone in his sector to begin firing at the same time. Our approaching aircraft then flew through this curtain of the barrage-sector fire.

The flak curve chart that was developed for all of us flying over enemy territory showed that as the aircraft speed increased from two hundred and fifty knots to four hundred and fifty knots, the chances of getting hit decreased. Interestingly, as the speed increased past the four hundred and fifty knot level, the odds of taking a hit increased. That would happen because the aircraft was flying through more airspace in less time, with a constant rain of firing from the enemy. It seemed it was impossible to avoid being hit.

In January, 1967, we had a social get together in our bunkroom with numerous members of different squadrons in attendance. One of these officers was LTJG Frank Pendergast. Although not a naval aviator, he was an officer assigned to the Vigilante Squadron, RVAH-11, as a reconnaissance attack navigator (RAN). During our conversation, Frank told us he carried his own personal survival weapon. He then unzipped the pocket located on the left arm of his flight suit and produced a two-shot derringer pistol. He said if he was ever shot down, he might need to use it to escape. We all laughed and talked about the chances of ever getting an opportunity to use such a small weapon. Usually, when a plane was shot down over North Vietnam, the crew was captured very quickly, with little chance of escape.

On March 9, 1967, Frank was flying a mission just off shore from the Than Hoa area with the skipper of his squadron, Commander (CDR) Charles L. Putnam. Their call sign was Flint River 605. Suddenly, their aircraft was hit by long-range cannon fire from the Than Hoa area and burst into flames. The only choice they had was to eject, which they both did. During the ejection sequence of the Vigilante, Frank was the first to leave the aircraft, followed by the pilot, CDR Putnam. Putnam landed on the beach area and was presumed captured. Because Frank ejected first, he landed in the water several hundred yards short of the beach. Numerous jets from the Kitty Hawk observed the parachutes floating down and called for a search and rescue mission (SAR).

A flight of four "Sandys," the call sign for search and rescue helicopter escort in Vietnam (CSAR), received the search and rescue call. These Sandys operating off the carrier Ticonderoga were Skyraiders, nicknamed Spads, and came right up to provide assistance. Whenever you heard the call sign Sandys used over the radio, you could be assured there was a flight of Spads close by, escorting a helicopter for a rescue mission. The Spads were huge, propeller-driven aircraft that could carry enormous amounts of ammunition, linger over the rescue area for long periods, and take tremendous amounts of abuse from anti-aircraft weapons. It was very effective at staying on station and providing cover for the downed airman and the helicopter during a rescue attempt.

Frank safely landed in the water and got free from all his parachute lines. But, he found himself standing in chest-deep water, watching two soldiers armed with AK 47s coming out to get him. When they arrived, each one grabbed an arm and began to drag him towards the shore line. Because he could see the Sandys heading towards him, he pretended that his leg was hurt, to delay being taken to the beach. When the Sandys arrived on scene, they set up their normal rescue flight pattern, which was known as a luff berry formation. This circular formation was very effective in keeping the enemy at bay because one aircraft was always in position to fire at them. Each time the Spad entered his dive, the two soldiers holding Frank would let go of his arms, hold the rifles over their heads, and go underwater.

This had happened several times when Frank looked up and saw the navy rescue helicopter (call sign Loose Foot) arriving in the area. As the chopper got closer to him, his captors once again let go of his arms and went underwater to hide. The Spads were shooting anything that moved on the beach. It was then that Frank made his decision to take action to escape. He unzipped his small pocket where he kept his derringer and pulled it out. When the first soldier came up from holding his breath, Frank shot him between the eyes, apparently killing him instantly. The second soldier came up shortly after that, and Frank punched him in his face, causing the rifle to fall into the water. He then began to wade as fast as he could in the waist-deep water toward the arriving helicopter and away from that soldier. Frank luckily was pulled to safety by the helicopter crew members.

The Spads continued to strafe the beach while the helicopter made its departure, heading back to the carrier. During the flight to the ship, one of the helicopter crew members asked Frank why he didn't shoot the other soldier with the remaining bullet. Frank was running on a very high level of adrenaline and said, "I–I don't know," and continued to drink the bottle of scotch provided to him by the crewmembers!

For his heroic actions, LTJG Pendergast was awarded the **Navy Cross** and was reassigned to Flight School in Pensacola, where he went on to become a naval aviator in August 1968. He was assigned to VA-66, flying the A-4 Skyhawk, until March 31, 1972, when he left the navy. He passed away on January 16, 1998.

Unfortunately, CDR Charles Putnam was killed. His remains were discovered and returned to US control on November 3, 1982.

Chapter 12

GATLIN GUNS; SQUADRON MATE
GOES MIA; TRAGEDY AT HOME

One of the weapons our Skyhawks carried was the navy's version of the Vulcan Gatlin gun that fired 20mm rounds at a very high rate of speed. This speed was generated by its six barrels, which were air cooled; these barrels allowed the gun to fire six thousand rounds per minute. The Skyhawk could carry two of these Gatlin guns, one under each wing, which gave it the capability of firing twelve thousand rounds per minute. We never fired twelve thousand rounds per minute as we only held the trigger down for about three to ten seconds at a time. Because the 20mm ammunition was so heavy, the guns were only loaded to about one half of capacity for each mission. This enabled the plane to return to the carrier and land within its prescribed weight restrictions should the guns jam.

On March 7, 1967, my wingman and I were given a reconnaissance mission near the mouth of the Haiphong Harbor. We were trying to find junks that could carry weapons into the port of Haiphong from China. We approached the harbor from the ocean side as there were several active SAM sites located in the Haiphong area that had a range of about fifteen miles. At twenty miles from the port, we found a large junk heading south, just about to make the turn into Haiphong Harbor.

My aircraft was armed with two Gatlin guns, and my wingman was carrying four pods of 2.75 rockets. Each of these weapons was especially deadly for use on troops, tanks, or other medium-protected targets. Because the Gatlin guns had such a high rate of fire and each 20mm individual projectile exploded when it hit the target, it was possible to destroy a tank with a short, five-second burst of fire. This occurred because there were so many rounds hitting the target within the same time period that it had a cumulative effect much greater than rounds spread out striking the same target.

We were coming in at a fairly low altitude of four thousand feet to avoid the radar coverage from the SAM sites. After we found the junk, we made a full circle, climbed up to eight thousand feet, and accelerated to three hundred and fifty knots. During the brief on the carrier, we had decided I would be rolling in first to strike the target while my wingman made another circle to observe the effects. We were both interested to see what kind of damage these Gatlin guns caused as neither one of us had every fired one in combat.

I took my time and got everything set up properly to attack the junk. As I rolled into a forty-five-degree dive, which was standard for delivering most of our weapon systems, my airspeed increased to four hundred and fifty knots. I pulled the trigger at forty-five hundred feet, watching fire leap ahead of the Gatlin guns ten to fifteen feet. The aircraft airspeed lost a hundred knots, decreasing to three hundred and fifty knots. Because of the deceleration caused by the recoil of the Gatlin guns, I found myself hanging in the shoulder harness about a foot ahead of the back of the ejection seat. I held the trigger down for about ten seconds, which was a long period of time while firing these weapons. I pulled out of the dive at around twenty-five hundred feet, which was lower than I would have done over land as the threat from anti-aircraft weapons was much greater there.

I was turning and climbing back up to a higher altitude when I looked down towards the junk's previous position. There was nothing of any size left. The largest piece of anything appeared to be about ten feet. Whatever the junk had intended to deliver into Haiphong Harbor was now at the bottom of the Gulf of Tonkin!

Another one of my roommates was Alexander J. Palenscar III, and he had the nickname of "Doc." Along with Jerry Hogan and myself, he had grown a mustache. The three of us had developed names of stash one, stash two, and I was stash three. As mentioned earlier, Doc and I traveled over to Naples, Italy, to join our squadron in January, 1966.

He was born on October 20, 1941, in Flushing, New York. His father was in the air force, and growing up, his family lived the typical service life, which included moving every few years. As a young boy, he would imitate Bugs Bunny with the saying, "What's up, Doc?" This is where he got the nickname that stayed with him all the way through the Naval Academy, from which he graduated in 1963, and throughout the rest of his life. I remember Doc explaining the Battle of Midway, Battle of the Coral Sea, and other historical naval events to me during our time spent together. As a person with very little military experience myself, I loved to listen to him explain the navy stories as I was impressed by his naval knowledge and his ability to bring life and detail to each story he told.

Doc was married, and like Sandy and myself, they lived on the base. They had a German Sheppard named Kaiser, and the four of us spent a lot of time together. For all those reasons, Doc was my closest friend of all our squadron naval aviators, and he epitomized the saying, "Duty, Honor, Country."

On March 27, 1967, Doc left our bunkroom to fly another mission. His flight of four Skyhawks were sent to destroy the Dao My highway bridge, located northwest of Vinh, North Vietnam. As it turned out, he was flying an A-4 with the side number of 415, which was the same number as Jerry Hogan's aircraft when he was lost on an earlier mission. Maintenance had re-numbered the aircraft to keep continuity in our small fleet of planes.

Doc was flying in the number four position, which made him the last Skyhawk to roll in and attack the bridge. It was unclear what happened to him as he called off the target and was never seen or heard from again. Initially, we all had hoped his radio failed and he had made it to feet wet as none of his flight members had seen a crash.

Back on board, carrier life continued to go on with no interruption in the evening movie or any other normal activity. This seeming lack of concern was to have a long-term negative effect on me. I never had any medical training to know what happened to me, and PTSD was unheard of during that time period. Suffice it to say, something "snapped" in my mind, forever changing the way I looked at losing someone close.

At dawn the next morning, many of our carrier pilots, including myself, began a major search operation. I was still in a state of shock, but I kept it to myself and flew the number four position in a division of A-4s, led by my flight leader LCDR Joe Eichinger. We were to comb the ocean by spreading out, in the hope of finding Doc.

Every naval aviator in combat carried a survival radio to communicate with search and rescue aircraft. Besides having a voice mode, these radios were equipped to send out an emergency SOS signal that could be heard by the searching aircraft. About midway through our sortie, my radio began to pick up one of these SOS signals that lasted for about five seconds. I reported it to Joe, and he asked if any other planes had picked up the signal. I was the only one who received the transmission, which was not that unusual as the signal can be very weak and each radio can be peaked at different levels of receiving.

We made many circles around the area where I had picked up the transmission, but none of us heard anything more. Because I heard the emergency transmission, our carrier continued to search for Doc for three more days, with no luck of finding him. At the end of the third day, word came down from operations that I had probably heard a signal coming from the DMZ area many miles away. I always thought that this would have been impossible, but it gave a reason to stop the search.

Doc was carried as MIA until the Secretary of the Navy approved a Presumptive Finding of Death in May 1973. On August 28, 1996, the remains thought to be his were turned over to the United States by the North Vietnamese. On November 4, 2002, bone analysis confirmed that the remains were his. On June 21, 2004, there was a funeral ceremony held at the Naval Academy, and many of his classmates from the academy attended.

His name is on the Vietnam Memorial Wall, panel 17E, line 059, and is inscribed on the Courts of the Missing at the Honolulu Memorial. He also has a memorial headstone in Arlington Cemetery, which was placed there before his remains were found.

To this day, I cannot understand why I heard the SOS signal over the water while we were searching for Doc. Is it possible that I wanted to find him alive so badly that my mind was playing a trick on me? Since his remains were found near the site that he had bombed, he obviously never made it to feet wet. Since stash one and stash two were now MIA, and no one without a mustache was being shot down, I shaved mine off just to be on the safe side.

Alexander Palenscar has been missed by his wife, children, and many of his close friends, including me. Doc was twenty-six-years-old when he was shot down and never had the chance to see his unborn son before he died.

We were just finishing our second line period on March 28, 1967, when I arrived back on board the Kitty Hawk after my second combat flight of the day. I was met by our skipper, and he asked me to come down to his stateroom. I dropped off my flight gear in my locker located adjacent to our ready room and went to the commanding officer's room. He showed me a telegram he had just received from my parents, who were living in Fort Myers, Florida.

My mother had been married to David Harper, her third husband, for over eight years. They had started a new family, which included having two children: one daughter, Belinda, age seven, and one son, Mark, age five. We were a close family, and when I left for Vietnam, they were very concerned for my safety as they knew the risks of flying combat missions over Vietnam.

When I read the telegram, I couldn't believe what it said. My parents and their children were visiting my grandmother, who lived in a beautiful home on a huge lot, surrounded by water on three sides. While my mom and David were inside talking with a group of family and friends, the children were outside playing. One of Mark's cousins came running into the house and told my parents that Mark had fallen into the water. All the adults went outside to help. It turned out that Mark had fallen into the only deep water that surrounded the property. They pulled his lifeless body back up on land and began giving him CPR. Unfortunately, it was not successful, and Mark was pronounced dead upon arriving at the hospital. Ironically, he had been scheduled to begin swimming lessons the next day.

My skipper told me to take emergency leave for up to thirty days, travel to Fort Myers, and attend the funeral. I flew an A-4 to Cubi Point and caught a plane to Clark Air Base, located in the Philippines. Fortunately, I was able to get out of Clark Air Base on a nonstop flight to San Francisco, where I connected with a flight to Tampa, Florida.

When I arrived in Tampa, I located my wife, who had just arrived from Lemoore. At about that same time, my cousin, Billy Smith, who had come up to take us to Fort Myers by car, found us. Four hours later, we were at my parent's house, finding them in a total state of shock.

During our visit with them, my Mom said she had been worried about me getting killed in Vietnam but never considered the possibility of losing Mark in some kind of accident. She was under a doctor's care and had been taking tranquilizers, which made her sleepy and hard to understand when she talked. This condition would continue for many years.

The funeral came and went with a lot of tears, as you can imagine. I was beginning to feel guilty about being away from my squadron mates as we were actively engaged in war. We had developed a tremendous feeling of esprit de corps among ourselves. Because I was on emergency leave and we had lost two naval aviators, it meant that the pilots left on board the carrier had to fly extra missions.

Even though Sandy tried to talk me into staying longer, I left to go back to Vietnam and arrived in the Philippines on April 10, 1967. The ship had already left Cubi Point to go back on the line, and I flew an A-4 out to the ship on April 11, being gone for a total of twelve days. On April 12th, I flew two combat missions over North Vietnam, never missing one day of combat duty! I would like to think my actions would have been approved by both Jerry and Doc as examples of Duty, Honor, Country.

Chapter 13
HAIPHONG POWER PLANT; KEP AIRFIELD RAID

The two A-4 squadrons aboard the Kitty Hawk were always selected to bomb the "sensitive targets." These targets were typically located in a downtown location, and any bombs that missed them could cause extensive collateral damage. As we bombed by sight (or visually), the chances of missing the target were much less than those planes that bombed by instruments using latitude and longitude coordinates.

For example, in 1965, the A-6 Intruders arrived in the Vietnam theater. They were an advanced bomber, using state-of-the-art techniques, like loading the target coordinates into the on-board computer. The A-6 would then fly to the target area and deliver the weapons on the target loaded into the computer prior to departing the carrier.

After several months of operations, it was determined that the A-6 squadrons were missing most of the targets they were trying to destroy.

The reason turned out not to be the aircraft system or the crew. The problem was the charts the crews were using. They had been created at a time when there were no sophisticated satellites, GPS, or other advance methods of mapping a country. To correct this problem, the air force was tasked with the responsibility of re-mapping the entire area of Asia where we were working. These countries included North and South Vietnam, Thailand, Laos, and Cambodia. On one of my missions over North Vietnam, I observed an SR-71 aircraft flying back and forth from one end of the country to the other. The SR-71 was our secret spy plane at the time. It was very fast, flew at high altitudes, and had the capability to map a geographical area. It was in the process of doing this when I saw the plane over North Vietnam. Shortly after sighting the SR-71, our A-6 aircraft began hitting their targets much more reliably, due to the new charts that arrived on board our carrier.

April 21, 1967, arrived, and we found our carrier teamed up with the carrier Ticonderoga and involved in the first Alpha strike on power plants located in the Haiphong area. Specifically, one power plant was located in the city itself, while the other one was located 2.1 miles northeast of the Haiphong commercial district on the south bank of the Cau Cam River. This second site was the one that I was involved in bombing using MK 81 bombs (two hundred and fifty pounds each).

The mission was briefed to be a flight of four Skyhawks supported by other aircraft from the carrier's air wing. We were to strike the power plant carefully, so as not to do any collateral damage to buildings in the immediate area. I remember being shot at more than normal due to being over the city of Haiphong, but we all returned safely. We located the target with ease and delivered our bombs right on target. Later, we discussed how we "neatly and surgically removed it from the face of the earth," and how "Haiphong was now dining by candle light."

Part of the following article appeared in the Jacksonville, Florida, newspaper on April 21, 1967, "City Hit First Time in War, Hanoi Says Attacks Serious Step of Escalation":

A swarm of U.S. Navy jets severely damaged a power plant within Haiphong and another on its outskirts in the war's first raid on the North Vietnamese port city, the U.S. command said Friday.

The raid Thursday left much of the surrounding area darkened in the night. In the forays against the Haiphong complex on Thursday, Navy fliers from two aircraft carriers in the Tonkin Gulf concentrated on the two Haiphong Power plants, flying through intense antiaircraft and missile fire. The carrier pilots attacked nine antiaircraft sites and thirteen missile sites in the Haiphong area, the Navy reported.

The power plant located outside the city was well within the suburbs, the U.S. command said. This plant furnished power for the city, its industry and port. Pilots said their bombing of this plant left Haiphong in darkness Thursday night. They reported the boiler house destroyed and the generator and transformer buildings damaged.

Rear Admiral David C. Richardson, commander of Task Force 77, told reporters the planes hit inside Haiphong, which we had not done before. Pilots said some of the bombs fell outside the target area, but none landed more than fifty feet away and the closest that any fell to houses was one hundred fifty to three hundred feet.

Pilots returning after dark from reconnaissance missions reported, that 'there were no lights tonight in Haiphong or Hon Gai,' a sister city twenty-seven miles to the northeast. The Navy declined, on grounds of security, to say exactly how many planes took part. There were, however, forty to fifty flights from the two carriers. One flight consists of three to five planes. This total included flak suppression and support aircraft.

Among pilots participating in the attack was LTJG Jules Harper of Fort Myers, Florida. His plane was in the second wave.

Navy officials, from Admiral Roy L. Johnson, commander in chief of the Pacific fleet who was aboard the Kitty Hawk, to the strike pilots themselves, emphasized the attacks were made with all possible precision in an effort not to inflict civilian casualties."

A decision was made to strike the Kep Air Field located thirty-seven miles north-east of Hanoi on April 24, 1967. It was an operational support base for Mig-15 and Mig-17 jets. The airstrip had been built by the Japanese in WW II.

The Kitty Hawk was forming a strike force of A-4 Skyhawk's from VA -144, A-6 Intruders from VA-85, and F-4 Phantoms from VF-213 and VF-214. VA-112 was to supply flak and SAM suppression missions for our fighters and bombers.

Karl Jarden and myself, acting as an Iron Hand element, were to lead the strike group north in our section of Skyhawks over the Gulf of Tonkin. As we were approaching Haiphong from offshore, the two of us were to break away from the strike group and turn west towards the city. The main strike group was to continue north and eventually turn west, just south of China, paralleling the border into the target area. We were to attack a known surface-to-air missile site located downtown that had been firing on our group three days prior as we were knocking out the two Haiphong power plants. This plan was to allow our main strike group to continue flying north at a higher altitude so they could conserve fuel to complete their missions.

An Iron Hand element was the name given to the aircraft group that was assigned to attack surface-to-air missile sites. Their job was to knock these sites out of commission so the attacking strike group would not have to be overly concerned with their threat. Iron Hand aircraft were typically loaded with the AGM 45 missiles. These missiles had a 2.5 pound warhead and were designed to damage the antennas, temporally taking them out of service. By comparison, the SAM had an eighty-six-pound warhead that could be exploded by impact or detonated by proximity.

Depending on the severity of the hostile environment the Iron Hand element was operating in, there were two delivery options. The first option of the approaching aircraft was to deliver the weapon three to five miles away from the target. This was accomplished by raising the nose of the aircraft approximately ten to twenty degrees and releasing the weapon in the general direction of the target. The AGM 45 missile would then proceed to the target area while climbing to a higher altitude. When the rocket motor ran out of fuel, the missile would be pulled back to the ground by gravity. It was equipped with a guidance system that would lock on to the specific signals from the surface-to-air missile radar site or the anti-aircraft radar site and track it down to its antennae. This technique was safer to use than the next option.

"Fire down the throat" was the second method of delivering the AGM 45 missiles. If the location of the SAM sites were known, the Iron Hand element could fly directly to them, roll into a forty-five-degree dive position, and fire the missile straight into the enemy antennas. This method allowed the aircraft to be less than a mile directly above the threat site and have a better chance of delivering the AGM 45 missile into the target, thereby taking it out of service.

Karl and I knew the North Vietnamese would still be hurting from our previous raids, and they would want another chance to destroy any American planes that would venture into their airspace. Since there were only going to be the two of us flying around downtown Haiphong, our expectations were that we were going to be shot at by everyone who had any kind of a weapon.

As accurate as the SAM was, it did have a weakness. If you could fly your aircraft into a position less than three miles from the center of the SAM site and circle that position, the SAM site operator would not have enough time to give steering commands to the missile, enabling it to hit you.

We briefed the Iron Hand mission to fly into the area as fast as our Skyhawks would go, which was a little over five hundred knots. As we approached three miles from the SAM site, we would trade our airspeed for a higher altitude to arrive in an attack position at eight thousand feet. We knew we would be separated because of all the anti-aircraft gun fire and because we could not see what was happening directly behind our jets. We planned to use the luff berry tactic. As you recall, this tactic consisted of each aircraft positioning itself on the other side of the three-mile circle so we could see and call out warnings to each other.

This was my seventy-fourth mission, and I was beginning to understand what was going to happen. My experience level was increasing as we were flying at least once and sometimes twice daily. All the aircraft that were flying these missions were on the same radio frequency. Everyone was briefed to maintain radio silence unless you needed to call out enemy aircraft, anti-aircraft fire, or SAMs.

Karl and I broke away from the strike group as we had briefed. As we approached the city of Haiphong, we came under intense anti-aircraft fire. Somehow we each flew through it and arrived at the SAM site as planned.

As I was approaching my roll-in point to attack the SAM site, I saw a missile being launched from the site aimed directly at me. I rolled into my forty-five-degree dive, using the fire down the throat technique, fired one of my AGM 45 missiles directly at the antennae site. The two missiles, each going a different direction, passed close abeam each other in flight. The SAM came so close to me I could easily see the Russian lettering on its side. I broke away from the incoming missile and pulled out of my dive while being shot at by most of the population of Haiphong.

Karl was approaching his roll-in point when the missile site fired a SAM at him. He delivered his weapon on the site, pulled up off the target, and watched the missile pass harmlessly by his aircraft. We continued our attacks and constant verbal communications with each other on the radios. I remember how dry my throat became. Adrenaline kicked in as missiles were coming at us from an additional location, and when they missed our aircraft, their operators blew them up, sending huge pieces of metal down upon the city and residents of Haiphong. This attack continued until six missiles had been fired at Karl and six missiles had been fired at myself. The two of us flew out of Haiphong and, miraculously, suffered no battle damage.

The rest of the strike group continued into the Kep area and reported doing moderate damage to the seven thousand-foot runway, control tower, maintenance building, and other support buildings. They also reported destroying a number of flak sites, surface-to-air missile sites, and aircraft revetment areas. Two Mig-17s were downed by F-4 Phantom pilots from VF-114 who provided fighter cover for the attacking A-6s and A-4s.

We lost one A-6 Intruder that was shot down by a Mig fighter. The crew ejected safely. Upon reaching the ground and prior to being captured by the North Vietnamese, the pilot took out his emergency hand-held radio and transmitted warnings to his previous wingman about Migs coming up behind him.

During the egress, an F-4 Phantom had a malfunction in its fuel system that required ejection over the Gulf of Tonkin. Both the pilot and radar intercept officer were picked up in good shape by one of our rescue helicopters.

During the debriefings, the pilots reported that the flak, Mig, and SAM activity was the worst they had ever encountered. As a side note, they concluded that listening, on the common radio frequency, to Karl and myself attacking the missile site in Haiphong was one of the scariest parts of the mission!

For my participation in this raid, I was awarded the **Navy Commendation Medal**.

Citation

In the name of the Secretary of the Navy, the Commander in Chief U.S. Pacific Fleet takes pleasure in awarding the **Navy Commendation Medal** *to LTJG Julian Harvey Harper, USNR.*

For heroism and extraordinary achievement while participating in aerial flight as pilot of a jet aircraft attached to Attack Squadron One Hundred Twelve, embarked in USS Kitty Hawk (CVA-63) during a strike against the heavily defended Kep Airfield, North Vietnam on 24 April 1967. LTJG Harper was wingman of a flight of two A-4s assigned to suppress the surface-to-air missile threat originating from the Haiphong area in support of the first coordinated Air Wing strike against Kep Airfield.

While skillfully maneuvering his aircraft into a shielding position for the oncoming main strike group, he drew the fire of persistent enemy anti-aircraft weapons. Twice, during the main strike group's attack on the target, LTJG Harper was brought under direct attack by surface-to-air missiles from two active sites. Despite the oncoming missiles, which resulted in two near misses, he resolutely maneuvered to deliver his ordnance on the firing sites, silencing both for the duration of the strike group's retirement. Through his outstanding airmanship and perseverance in the face of intense enemy fire, LTJG Harper contributed substantially to the success of the strike and safe return of the strike group. His courage and skill were in keeping with the highest traditions of the United States Naval Service. LTJG Harper is authorized to wear the Combat "V."

Signed by Roy L. Johnson, Admiral, U.S. Navy.

Chapter 14
R AND R; HANOI RAID

After four weeks operating on Yankee Station, the Kitty Hawk left the Gulf of Tonkin and headed back to Cubi Point in the Philippines for two weeks of well-deserved R and R.

The Kitty Hawk Cruise Book, which was published each cruise, had this to say about the Philippines:

The Republic of the Philippines is a vast array of over ten thousand islands sprinkled throughout the western portion of the Pacific. In the past this country has been subject to a variety of regimes some of which helped the cultural development while others tended to impair or stunt this country's progress.

The islands are landscaped with rich green tropical plants and drenched with the sun's subtropical heat. The ruins of ancient fortresses stand as tacit reminders of conflicts between men of earlier generations.

The island of Luzon, where the capital city of Manila is located, serves as a temporary home port to Kitty Hawk while she is deployed to Westpac. The in-port period is always a pleasant relief after the strain and monotony of an extended period of at-sea operations.

Cubi Point is located in Subic Bay and has some interesting history. Towards the end of World War II, we had a huge number of military jeeps in the Philippines. When the war was over, our government had to decide what to do with them. As I recall the story, they ordered all of the remaining American jeeps in the Philippines destroyed. They did not want to have them brought back into America for economic reasons. This was accomplished by putting them on barges and taking them out into Subic Bay and pushing them overboard. The Filipinos had their empty barges out in the same bay. Because there was nothing wrong with the jeeps, when the Americans pushed them over the side, the Filipinos sent divers down to hook a line on the jeeps and raise them up onto their barges. This is how there came to be so many colorful Jitneys running around the Philippines.

Our base at Cubi Point was very well situated. The carrier tied up at the dock, which was located within walking distance to the airfield, complete with all the hangers that provided maintenance for our aircraft. Because it was staffed by our own American personnel, it had all the conveniences of a naval air station located in America. It was always fun to fly a plane into Cubi Point because after you secured your aircraft, the plane captain would hand you an ice cold can of beer!

Directly in front of where the carrier berthed was a navy special services area where you could check out sixteen-foot sailboats for the day. Obviously, you had to qualify by demonstrating you knew how to operate a sailboat. Once I qualified, I spent many hours sailing around Subic Bay, which I understand is now a fabulous resort area.

One of the places you could sail to and visit was Grand Island. It was located just to the west of the base across the entrance to the harbor. The navy had set it up with a beautiful beach atmosphere, and all station naval personnel, both enlisted men and officers, could go to relax for the day. Fortunately for our air wing, we were also included. You could get hamburgers, steaks, beer, and many other items that you might want. If you weren't fortunate enough to be able to sail to the island, the base ran a small ferry boat back and forth, making it easy to visit.

Should you want to leave the base, you left on Magsaysay Boulevard and crossed the polluted Olongapo River. There were young children swimming in the water, and they would dive down to retrieve any coins you threw in for them. Once you crossed the bridge, you found yourself in Olongapo City. Olongapo was just one street after another lined with bars. Since the average age of the military men visiting Olongapo was about twenty years old, you can understand it had the reputation of being an adult Disneyland!

For the air wing naval aviators, we spent most of our time at the local officers' club. My favorite drink was a stinger on the rocks, which was made with brandy and crème de menthe poured over ice. The price for any drink in the club was only twenty-five cents, so you can imagine how it was possible to be over-served.

One night most of our air wing officers were in the club, and after several hours of drinking, we devised a game we called "dead bat." The object of this new game was to hang upside down from the open rafters supporting the roof of the clubhouse. The first one to come down had to buy a round of drinks for the remaining dead bat participants.

It was a loud and rowdy collection of pilots. The base duty officer had been called, and when he arrived, he asked all of us to come down from the rafters, which none of us did. Shortly, the captain of the base arrived and ordered the senior officer present to present himself. Commander of the air group (CAG) came swinging down from the rafters and saluted the captain of the base. Words were exchanged between the two officers, and the result was that the club was closed, and we all followed CAG back to the ship. Even on liberty (time off), we had esprit de corps!

While we were in port, Tom Baggett, one of the naval aviators who lived in the junior officers' bunkroom, began to compose songs about our experiences flying combat missions over Vietnam. He had a twelve string guitar and could play many songs very well.

Using the music of songs already published, he added his own words to the tunes. For example, he used the tune of the song "Red River Valley" to tell of our missions over Hanoi. After we destroyed the Haiphong power plant, he wrote and sang a song about the city of Haiphong dining by candle light. He even wrote one song about our game of dead bat that had occurred in the officers' club at Cubi Point.

Tom went on to write numerous other songs and recorded them all on a tape. He sent them back to a publisher in the United States, and after waiting for about two months, he received a reply from the publisher. As I recall, it went something like this: "Dear LTJG Baggett, as you are well aware of the sentiment in the United States about the Vietnam Conflict, your songs go against the overwhelming desire of the American people to get our country out of this conflict. Really, LTJG Baggett, our country is not ready for your songs."

Tom read us this letter, and we discussed it several different times in our bunkroom. We all thought it was interesting that the Americans who were protesting our involvement in the Vietnam War had free access to the press and that the press seemed to have very little interest in what our military was doing in Vietnam.

All of us in the bunkroom continued to hear Tom sing his songs for the rest of the cruise, as well as for the second cruise. Tom left the navy after his first five-year commitment and went back to college and received a law degree. He practiced law and also went to work for United Airlines as an airline pilot. Unfortunately, Tom died at a fairly young age. His recorded songs were put on a CD and sent to all the remaining VA-112 squadron pilots. They are still being enjoyed by all of us.

We left Cubi Point in time to arrive on Yankee Station to begin flying on May 9, 1967. This was the last month of our cruise that we were scheduled to be flying missions against North Vietnam. The weather had cleared up tremendously, and we began to hit a lot of different targets. I wrote the following press releases that describe some of our squadron's activity during this time period, and they were published in my home town newspaper, the *Fort Myers New Press*.

May 14, 1967: A flight of Skyhawk jets smashed a shipping facility in North Vietnam about ten miles south of Thanh Hoa. "There was a pier next to a warehouse and several barges along the bank of the river in the target area," one of the pilots, LTJG Jules Harper of Fort Myers, FL reported.

"I rolled in behind the leader and saw his rockets scorch the barges. I followed him and fired my rockets, pulled off, and saw them streaking towards the targets. As I looked back, the warehouse was burning, the pier was down and three barges were smoking."

LTJG Mike Gump of Tucson, Arizona, reported, "As I pulled out, I rolled over on my back and saw the warehouse was blazing and columns of black smoke were rising from it."

May 17, 1967: The VA-112 Broncos, led by their skipper CDR Lee Minnis, of Dallas, Tex., destroyed two trucks and severely damaged another one twenty-six miles northwest of Dong Hoi. "The skipper found some camouflaged trucks near Gap Mui Ron," recalled LT Don Gerrish of Terre Haute, Ind. "My bombs scared them back on the road, and the rest of the flight's bombs covered them. They were still burning when we left."

Other VA-112 pilots found a string of barges tied together and splintered them with two hundred fifty and five hundred pound bombs. LTJG Jules Harper remarked, "As I pulled off the target and looked back, I could see several barges lift up in the air and debris flying everywhere."

May 18, 1967: LCDR Jim Lucchesi of Jacksonville led a flight of Navy pilots in the bombardment Sunday of a North Vietnamese truck convoy.

Sent out from the aircraft carrier Kitty Hawk, the planes pounded the main north-south highway in North Vietnam and then spotted twenty to thirty camouflaged trucks heading south. "They were hard to see, but the lead aircraft (Lucchessi) placed his bombs right in the area," said LTJG Jules Harper of Fort Myers. "I dropped my bombs and then we circled around to strafe what was left of the group."

On May 19, 1967: Our carrier participated in a multi carrier Alpha strike against the Van Dien Army Supply Depot near Hanoi. The first strike was led by the executive officer of VA-85, CDR Jerry Putter, of Phoenix, Arizona. The second coordinated wave of the strike, which I participated in, was led by VF-114's executive officer CDR Joe Johnson, of Biloxi, Mississippi.

My roommate LCDR Bob Saville and I were assigned the mission of Iron Hand. We were to lead our second group into the Hanoi area and suppress the SAM fire using the shrike missiles like I used in the Kep Raid. There were so many surface-to-air missile sites in the Hanoi vicinity we knew our missiles would lock onto one of the radar signals easily and track it down to its antenna. Therefore, we planned to use the safer delivery method of firing the shrikes three to five miles out from the target by raising our aircraft nose ten to fifteen degrees before launching the missiles.

During the brief, we were looking for something that would make this mission seem safer. Hanoi was by far the most dangerous Vietnamese city to fly over. We discussed the fact that even though we were ahead of all the other aircraft on our strike, and the first ones to be fired on by the enemy, at least our aircraft didn't smoke. The A-4C, which had the J-65 engine, was the only jet aircraft aboard our carrier that did not put black smoke out of its tail pipe while it was flying. This was a huge advantage for operating our Skyhawks during daylight hours over enemy territory. Our plane was so small, it was difficult to be seen by the naked eye but could be observed by radar, and Hanoi was rich in radar-controlled, anti-aircraft gun sites.

On almost all my combat missions, I carried a super 8 movie camera and took pictures of what was going on. Many of my fellow pilots took their still cameras along to do the same. The men in my airframes division had created a camera mount that was attached to the glare shield of the Skyhawk to hold my camera during flight. I took over two thousand feet of combat movies during my time in Vietnam, which included a picture of a SAM flying right across the front of my aircraft. Bob and I briefed each other on trying to get some pictures over the Hanoi area as we knew there would be a lot of action. Because of the threat of Migs on this mission, both our fighter squadrons were going to be protecting us by intercepting any hostile aircraft in the region. Normally, one of the fighter squadrons would have been armed with bombs. The problem was that only one of the fighter squadrons had IFF capability, which means the ability to identify us as friend or foe. The other squadron had to rely on visual identification, and in combat, that could be tricky.

The twenty-five-plus aircraft we were leading went feet dry just south of Thanh Hoa. We continued on a westerly heading until we were directly south of Hanoi; then we turned to the north and proceeded to the target area. As we got to within about ten miles of Hanoi, we passed the exiting wave of attacking aircraft from the other carrier's strike group. Some of the aircraft were below us, and some were above us. I had my head on a swivel, as we used to say, to see as much as I could of what was going on around me. Directly ahead I saw an F-4 Phantom from the other carrier going straight up in the air, trying to outrun a SAM that was catching him from beneath. The Phantom was a very fast aircraft, but the SAM could obtain speeds up to 2.5 Mach, which was much faster than the top speed of the Phantom. The missile caught up with the F-4, and when it exploded, the Phantom was destroyed. Fortunately, both crewmembers ejected and were floating down in their parachutes as we came flying by them. I could not believe what I was seeing as the machine gun tracer's bullets were passing by both the pilot and RIO as they were descending. Apparently, it was normal for the gunners to try and kill you while you were in the air. Once you touched the ground, they took you prisoner of war.

Al Lee, one of our squadron pilots who was also on the mission, took still pictures of this event, and we all looked at the photos when we got back aboard the ship. You could clearly see the tracer bullets going by one of the crewmembers. The question was raised in our discussion about how the North Vietnamese know if they are shooting at an American pilot or a Mig pilot. The answer was that the North Vietnamese Mig pilots had a darker colored parachute than the Americans.

Things happen fast in a jet! I had just finished seeing this gruesome site when I heard an explosion, felt a concussion in my ears, and found myself flying in my A-4 upside down, starring at anti-aircraft gun muzzle flashes from the ground. I moved the aircraft's control stick over to the side and righted the airplane. Bob broke radio silence and asked if I was all right, to which I replied in the affirmative. The SAM that had just missed me blew up one hundred and fifty feet behind my aircraft, just as the ALQ-51 electronic counter measures (ECM) gear had directed it to do. I had a quick thought: *Thank you, Singer Sewing Machine Company!*

One of our F-4 Phantoms that was not equipped with identify friend or foe (IFF) was trailing us. He came over the radio and said he had a skin paint of several airplanes directly ahead of him. The other IFF-equipped F-4 came back and told him he was painting the Iron Hand element, which was us, and we were not Migs. I was hoping that statement was enough to keep us from being shot with a Sidewinder missile from the Phantom pilot making the comment about having a skin paint.

We finally came into firing range for our missiles and launched them at the target area, hoping they would do what they were designed to accomplish. Bob and I then reversed course and headed back to feet wet. One of our squadron pilots, LCDR Cliff Ruthrauff, entered his dive and found himself looking at the wrong target. At great risk to himself, he pulled out of his dive run with his bombs still on board. He circled around while climbing back to the correct altitude to begin another dive bombing run, all while taking continuous anti-aircraft gun fire. Bomb damage photographs taken after the raid showed that his assigned target had been completely destroyed. His actions proved to me the professionalism of our pilots as he could have dropped his bombs on the wrong building and departed for the safety of feet wet.

For this mission, I received another **Navy Commendation Medal**.

Citation

In the name of the Secretary of the Navy, the Commander in Chief U.S. Pacific Fleet takes pleasure in awarding a Gold Star in lieu of the **Second Navy Commendation Medal** *to LTJG Julian Harvey Harper, United States Naval Reserve for service as set forth below:*

For heroic achievement while serving as a pilot of a jet aircraft attached to Attack Squadron ONE HUNDRED TWELVE, embarked on USS KITTY HAWK (CVA 63) engaged in combat operations against the North Vietnamese forces on 19 May 1967. LTJG Harper was wingman in a section of A-4 aircraft providing surface-to-air missile suppression for a coordinated Air Wing strike on the Van Dien Army Supply Depot near Hanoi. Doggedly maintaining position on his leader in spite of search and defensive maneuvers in an area continually threatened by intense surface-to-air missile and heavy anti-aircraft artillery activity, he fired his weapons into two active SAM sites. While attacking in section, one SAM burst close aboard and three others were sighted but were completely evaded. After the final weapon delivery against the enemy sites, the missile was seen to impact on the target and the signal ceased signifying probable target destruction. LTJG Harper's courage, outstanding airmanship and loyal devotion to duty were in keeping with the highest traditions of the United States Naval Service. LTJG Harper is authorized to wear the Combat "V."

Besides flying combat missions, I had also flown test hops, ferry trips back and forth to Cubi Point, and other non-combat sorties. As a result of all my flights, I had become a Kitty Hawk Centurion (one hundred carrier landings) on May 10, 1967. This was quite an accomplishment in itself! My last combat mission, number eighty-eight, of the first cruise was flown on May 22, 1967, and that was also the last day the ship was on the line. Our entire squadron celebrated as much as you could on an aircraft carrier that evening. The next day, May 23rd, most of our pilots flew our Skyhawks off the ship, taking them directly to Naha, Okinawa, and then over to Atsugi, Japan. This was done to get them repainted in the colors of the next arriving squadron. The combat A-4s stayed in the area, and we flew home to Lemoore aboard a commercial World Airways flight.

Chapter 15

THOMAS E. PETTIS STORY;
HOME AT LEMOORE

homas E. Pettis was a classmate of mine during our initial training in Pensacola, Florida, in 1964. For the sixteen weeks we were in training together, I knew him as Ed Pettis. He was from Mobile, Alabama, and was born on October 21, 1941. Going through all that training together, you get to know each other pretty well. Ed had a habit of biting his fingernails into the quick.

We graduated in class number five together and, afterwards, went our separate directions. Ed went to helicopters, and I didn't see him again until May of 1967 on-board the Kitty Hawk. He had come over from the USS Hornet. We had a chance to talk for about thirty minutes before he had to return to his carrier. I noticed he still had his nail biting habit. It was great to see him again after all the events that had taken place since our graduation together in 1964.

On May 23, 1967, LTJG Pettis was flying co-pilot on an SH-3A helicopter. He was flying with LT Richard W. Homuth, the captain of the helicopter, and two other crew members.

As I recall, they had been assigned a dangerous search and rescue mission to pick up two downed airmen who had successfully ejected out of an F-4 Phantom over North Vietnam. Normally, the SH-3A did not venture into North Vietnam as it was just too dangerous for the slow-flying helicopter. The mission was approved at the highest level as they knew the downed flyers were evading the North Vietnamese. They made this decision because they felt confident the rescue helicopter could find them as they knew their exact location.

The A-4s provided rescue assistance (rescap, as it was called) to the helicopter, and I followed the mission very carefully as it concerned my friend Ed Pettis. The plan was to go into North Vietnam in the direction of the downed airman. There was a known 37mm gun site in route to them. Four of the A-4s were planning to protect the helicopter by separating their flight interval in a circle so that one Skyhawk was aiming at the ground continuously to fire at any hostile targets that got in the way of the mission.

The A-4s were also going to help and direct the helicopter crew navigate to the downed airman as they were not used to navigating over North Vietnam. They had discussed using the radio to communicate instructions for doing this. The flight proceeded normally until shortly after going feet dry. Ed's helicopter was approaching the known 37mm site and was not making the planned turn to avoid it. The A-4s initially talked to the helicopter crew in a calm voice, instructing them to turn to the right to avoid the gun site. Unfortunately, they did not respond to that communication. The flight leader of the Skyhawks then began to frantically scream instruction to the helicopter crew, but to no avail.

As the helicopter got within range of the 37mm gun site, the gunners on the ground opened up on them, and according to the A-4 rescap aircraft, the bullets hit the rotor blades, shattering them into hundreds of pieces. This caused the helicopter to fall from the sky and crash into the ground. It was a violent impact and appeared to the Skyhawk pilots that no one could have survived the crash. No radio transmissions were heard from the helicopter crew during this entire time.

Once again, in combat situations, no one but the crew knew what happened in the aircraft. In Ed's case, a simple radio failure could have doomed the whole operation. Whether it was hit with a bullet fired up from the ground or just picked that particular time to fail, the result was the same.

LTJG Thomas E. Pettis's name is located on the Vietnam Wall. He is listed on panel 20E, Row 91. His remains were never returned to the United States.

Lemoore Naval Air Station, located in the state of California, was the master jet attack base for the West Coast of the United States. All of the Wes Pac squadrons were based there, and the dependents lived close to one another in base housing. While we were in Vietnam, our wives and families were awaiting news of what was happening to us. Our mail service was subject to weather delays, maintenance delays, etc., and, of course, there was no e-mail or satellite phone service. As a result, sometimes the wives would go days without receiving any letters.

I sent home a picture of the combat damage to my A-4; Sandy was shocked to see the extent of damage to the plane. She told me later that she knew I must be all right because there were several letters there for her to read that were written with a later stamp date than the envelope containing the picture.

As in any war, there were casualties. When a naval aviator was listed MIA or killed in action, the base commander, according to base policy, would send out an officer from his office, along with the base chaplain, to inform the wife of what had occurred. They would arrive together, being driven in one of the navy's black cars, at the wife's house. Since the houses were built together in a quad fashion, it was easy to know what was going on in your neighbor's home. As the war progressed, Sandy and the other wives would pray that the navy's black car would not stop in their quad. If it did stop, they could only hope the men would not come to their door. To put this in perspective, there were days when the chaplain and the other officer would visit two or three wives in a day, due to our loss rate of naval aviators from all the different squadrons on duty in Vietnam. When Sandy told me these stories, I felt it was easier to be actively engaged in combat than to be waiting back in Lemoore for news of what was happening in the war.

It was wonderful to be back in the States, and Sandy and I enjoyed getting back together again. We spent a lot of time socializing with other squadron members and their families as there was not much of an opportunity to get to know many other people. Sandy had finished teaching kindergarten, which she really enjoyed. Because her college major was in science, she had been reassigned to teach sixth grade science and English for the upcoming school year and spent part of the summer getting her lesson plans ready.

After taking most of the month of June off, I began my training cycle to prepare to go back to war in November. There were several of us selected to participate in a JTF-2 exercise. The initials stood for Joint Task Force. This exercise was conducted in Little Rock, Arkansas, and we were allowed to be accompanied by our wives.

The USN test director, Captain E. R. Hanks, and Winton R. Close, Major General, USAF Commander, JTF-2, were in charge of the program. The test was to determine which type of aircraft, either single-pilot or multi-pilot, could fly an extremely low-altitude, prescribed course. The pilot reported into an on-board cockpit recorder, which was analyzed to determine who saw the most as the flight progressed. The altitude they were talking about flying was fifty feet, which was what the A-4 pilots had trained at all their careers. I believe this gave us an advantage over the rest of the pilots who were flying different aircraft, especially those flying the fighter-type planes. The course consisted of a race track pattern approximately five hundred miles in length and had been set up with many fake (or dummy) troops, tanks, and other military items along its path. The data was reviewed once we got back to the base and would help the military decide what type of aircraft to build in the future.

I flew the course twice, first on August 2nd and then on August 4th. It turned out to be a lot of fun. I heard the A-4s had done better than either the F-4s or the A-6s, which had a crew of two instead of just one. One of the other squadron A-4 pilots had passed under a section of high power lines during his mission, and his aircraft's rudder had cut one of them, causing the wire to fall to the ground. This disrupted power over three different states, making quite a mess, and was reported on the national nightly news. My mother, who had just seen the news report, asked me, "Don't you pilots ever do anything that is safe?"

After Little Rock, we headed back to Lemoore to continue our training. Shortly after we got home, I found myself in a cockpit simulator, receiving a check ride by one of our squadron pilots. The ride did not go very well, and the instructor, Lieutenant Don Gerrish, was trying to debrief me in a professional manner on what I had done wrong. He could tell I was not listening very well and asked me what I thought. I looked at him and gave an unprofessional, smart-ass answer, "What are you going to do, send me back to Vietnam if I don't get it right?" I believe he had a little chat with our commanding officer about the incident, but I never heard anything else about it.

We flew many different types of training sorties during our brief stay at Lemoore, not all of them professional. As I'm sure you can tell by now, naval aviators like to have a good time, and it comes in forms that aren't always appropriate. That could be an understatement. The following are a few examples of the more playful flights in which I managed to be involved.

One night, during a mission over the Sierra Nevada Mountain range, I looked over to the east, and because it was late in the evening, Highway 395 that runs north and south through Bishop, California, was fairly vacant of traffic. There were a few cars, but they were spread out by several miles. I talked with my wingman on the radio, and we decided to have a little fun. We would turn off all our navigation lights, slow down to about one hundred and fifty knots, and roll into a gentle dive, aiming in the direction of one of those lone cars that was traveling north. At about three thousand feet above the ground in my shallow dive, I turned on the single landing light and aimed it straight at the car. I continued the dive until I reached one thousand feet above the ground, with the car directly in front of me. I then turned off the landing light and climbed back to higher altitude. My wingman was doing the same maneuver but was about a minute behind me. I'm sure the driver of the car reported a UFO sighting.

On a day mission over the Sierras, two of us were flying north at a low altitude, just looking for wildlife. Deer were the most common animals we could see as we flew over them at four hundred knots. As we approached a lake, there was a water skier being pulled by a pretty little boat. We had enough time to descend down to about ten to twenty feet above the lake before we passed just to the right of the skier, rocking our wings. As we climbed up to a higher altitude, we looked in our mirrors and saw that the skier had fallen. We circled around and watched as he climbed back into the boat unharmed.

Another interesting thing we did occurred on the way to Fallon, Nevada, where we went to practice our weapon deliveries. The two of us were flying in a loose section formation enjoying the view at about a one thousand feet above the ground. As we approached Mono Lake, which is located thirteen miles east of Yosemite National Park, near the town of Lee Vining, California, we saw a convertible car with the top down parked on a dirt road close to the lake. Mono Lake is a state park and is very isolated. My wingman and I were very young; I was twenty-four-years-old at the time. We both saw the car at about the same time and immediately looked at each other and obviously thought the same thing. We both gave the visual signal with our hands to begin a dive down towards the ground. Our speed increased to over five hundred knots, and we passed directly over the convertible at about fifty feet.

Our suspicions were confirmed as we could see a couple in the back seat doing what people do in the back seat of a convertible when they are in a desolate area. Over a beer that night, my wingman and I talked about what we had seen. We decided that it was probably the best sex either of the people would every have—or it might have been the worst!

Our squadron arrived in Fallon, Nevada, during the month of August, 1967. We worked on our delivery methods, not only for conventional weapons but also for nuclear. Every dive run we made was graded and scored. We dropped a little bomb known as the MK-76. It had the same aerodynamic characteristics of one of our regular bombs. The only explosive material in the MK-76 was a shotgun-shell-type device that exploded on impact, creating a white smoke signal, which could be seen from our aircraft or on the ground by the range officers.

After several days of dropping these practice bombs, we were graded and judged by numerous range officers. On August 26, 1967, I received the **Commander Fleet Air Alameda Excellence Award**.

Citation

LTJG Julian Harper, USNR, is hereby awarded an "E" in Dive Bombing—Minimum Altitude Release—in recognition of his outstanding Flight Performance as a member of Squadron VA-112 during competitive exercise A-7-R in A-4C aircraft at NAAS FALLON on 26 August 1967.

I really thought it was easier to do all this bombing here in the states with no one shooting at you, but I realized I would be back in Vietnam in the near future.

In the morning, one half of our squadron would fly, and the other half would be involved in other activities. One of the mornings I was not flying, nine of us from the squadron went to the rifle and pistol range. We had been assigned to work with a special training officer President Johnson had personally sent to Fallon to work with combat flight crews. Prior to this event, the only reason I carried my 38 pistol was to shoot flares up in the air to get the attention of searching aircraft. Our instructor assured us by the end of the morning we would all be able to hit a man at a range of one hundred yards, five out of five times. Everyone there laughed as we were all in the same category of pistol shooters: not good The range had a silhouette of a man standing up at one hundred yards away from the firing position. The instructor had us stand back about ten yards from the firing position, and when he gave the signal, we were to run up and fall down in a prone position. We were all wearing our flight suits that had numerous pockets. I carried my extra ammunition in the top pocket of the flight suit. When the signal was given, I ran forward and fell in a prone position, watching all my extra ammunition go sailing out of the pocket.

Feeling really stupid, I looked around and found I was not alone in losing my ammunition. Several of my buddies were in the same situation. The instructor had a few choice words for all of us as he had seen this happen before. Then he gave us the methods to use to hit a target at a hundred yards. After a few tries, we all mastered the art of shooting that little pistol and, in fact, did graduate by hitting the target five out of five times at a distance of a hundred yards. This was an amazing accomplishment, and to this day, I can't believe we all did it.

When night arrived each evening, we all headed to downtown Fallon to keep up with our drinking skills. Numerous casinos were run and controlled by an "old woman" we all lovingly called Ma. She personally trained many naval aviators in the art of gambling. I was one of her students, and, of course, I bought her casino chips. I lost them, but I did learn a lot about craps and black jack. Years later, when Ma died, there were several squadrons of aviators on deployment, practicing bombing in Fallon. The story I heard was they all got together and flew their planes in a fly over in her honor during the funeral. I occasionally think of her even as I gamble to this day.

Shortly before we left on our second cruise to Vietnam, we found out Sandy was pregnant, and her due date was projected to be a week or so before we returned in early June. The navy had a saying: "We are only in town long enough to lay the keel, then it's back to sea we go."

Chapter 16
SECOND WEST PAC CRUISE; FIRST LINE PERIOD; KHE SANH

We said goodbye to the states on November 18, 1967, and encountered smooth sailing going to Hawaii. Once again, several of our evaporators malfunctioned, and the fresh water was shut off shortly after leaving port. I remember joking that at least the ship had a good supply of deodorant at a good price. Fresh water is required to operate the steam catapults, and by turning a few valves, salt water can replace the fresh water being used in the showers and sinks. We could all continue to stay clean, but I can tell you that fresh water showering is much better than using salt water.

We arrived in Hawaii on November 23, 1967, and found it to be all James Michener had said it was—and more. Many of our squadron Broncos took the evening off and toured the nightlife before the ship left port the next day to commence the Operational Readiness Inspection. This inspection checked both conventional and nuclear readiness.

By this time in my brief navy career, I, along with several other squadron officers, were beginning to become very "salty." Salty is a naval expression that translates to being fairly senior in rank and knowing everything about any given subject. We had picked up several new naval aviators during our stay in Lemoore and had seen many of our fellow comrades depart for their new duty stations. These new arrivals were "boots," as I once had been on the Mediterranean cruise.

There was a humorous story about a salty pilot, a lieutenant, who was designated as a nuclear weapons loading officer. During an inspection at sea, one of the inspectors was paired up with this salty lieutenant. The job of the nuclear weapons loading officer was to take a crew of men to an aircraft, position the plane properly, and then oversee them loading a nuclear bomb on the plane. Each element of the exercise was graded, as were so many of the navy activities.

During this particular event, there were no planes, crews, or bombs, so the inspector told the lieutenant he was to simulate everything. The idea was to make sure the loading officer knew all the correct verbiage and procedures. The activity was to take place in the hanger bay. After a short meeting of the two officers, the inspector told the lieutenant to begin the exercise.

As the story went, the lieutenant began walking very slowly, issuing orders to his simulated crew on how to move the simulated aircraft. If you were just watching this operation, you would find if funny. The inspector was walking right behind the loading officer, taking notes on his every move. I mentioned the lieutenant was salty. He really thought he could be anywhere else, doing anything else, and be more productive than talking to his simulated crew, simulated plane, and simulated bomb. As the drill went on, the simulated aircraft continued to be moved to arrive at the correct position on the hanger deck for the simulated bomb to be loaded. Suddenly, the lieutenant stopped short of his destination. The inspector asked him, "Why did you stop?" The lieutenant answered,

"Sir, my simulated aircraft, being pushed by my simulated bomb crew, is having trouble getting over the fire door track on the hanger deck, sir." (The fire door tracks rise up a few inches, allowing the huge hanger doors to open or close in case of fire or for other operational reasons.) I can't imagine the grade that was given to this salty lieutenant, but I feel sure he got to practice this procedure several more times after his skipper read the inspection report!

Pulling back into Pearl Harbor on November 26th, all hands took advantage of a liberal liberty policy, taking special tours set up by the ship's Special Service Department. Waikiki, Diamond Head, the Blow Hole, and the Pali Lookout are sights never to be forgotten.

On November 30th, the ship was underway from Hawaii and set a course for Yokosuka, Japan. Skirting bad weather, we arrived in Tokyo Bay and Yokosuka with a magnificent view of famous Mount Fuji on December 8, 1967. Many squadron members finished their last-minute Christmas shopping there and visited such places as Tokyo, Kamakura, and Yokohama.

We said goodbye to Japan on December 12th, and the Philippines Islands were on the horizon on December 15th. We used the in-port period at Cubi Point for a last good liberty and to prepare our aircraft for the combat-line period, which was rapidly approaching. Unfortunately, a fire broke out in the carrier's tire locker and delayed our departure two additional days. I took the opportunity to check out a sail boat and sailed around the harbor area. I sailed right beside the ship where the fire was still burning and couldn't believe the view. The outside metal of the ship was a crimson red. Our men distinguished themselves with their efforts while fighting the blaze, and soon it was put out.

During our first and now our second combat cruise, Operation Rolling Thunder was the name of the campaign we were conducting our flight operations under. It consisted of a gradual and sustained bombing campaign of Vietnam, which began on March 2, 1965, and continued until November 1968. Some of the objectives we were most actively involved in were destroying North Vietnam's transportation system, air defenses, and industrial base and stopping the flow of material and men into South Vietnam. We were not as successful at this operation as we could have been, due to what I always called "step-by-step aggression." We had mentally been involved in a cold war for a long time, and our government was afraid that if we instituted a great deal of aggression all at one time against North Vietnam, Russia and China would react to it and possibly cause World War III. As it was, every time we would step up new attacks, Russia and China would send in more equipment and advisers to counter the new threat; they also sent more sophisticated weapons to shoot at our aircraft. US foreign policy did not go unnoticed by our pilots and was discussed at great lengths at night on-board the carrier.

We departed Cubi Point on December 21st and arrived on Yankee Station on December 23, 1967, which coincided with my first combat mission of the second cruise. My plane was loaded with five hundred-pound bombs, and I was sent into North Vietnam, south of Thanh Hoa, to find and destroy barges and any bridges I could locate. I was hampered by poor weather conditions that were normal for North Vietnam that time of the year. After searching around the area for far too long, I finally found some small barges and bombed them. Arriving back at the ship, I was amazed that I had not been hit by any anti-aircraft fire as there was plenty of it. It made me feel welcomed back in the war.

I flew one mission each day on the 24th through the 26th, two missions on the 27th, and to finish the year, one mission on December 28, 1967. Most of these missions were flown in poor weather conditions, which required us to fly some of them in South Vietnam. We could help our troops by working with a forward air controller, delivering our ordinance right on the enemy troops.

Meanwhile, our ordinance crews were having a lot of fun writing messages to the Communists on the bombs they were loading on our aircraft during the Christmas Season that would be "air mailed" to their recipients. Some examples were, "Merry Christmas, hope this bomb finds you in good health," and, the favorite, "Merry Christmas, Ho Chi Minh!" As leader of North Vietnam, Ho Chi Minh remained in power during both of our cruises to Vietnam. He died at age seventy-nine on September 2, 1969, over a year after we had departed the war area.

As I mentioned earlier, I flew one mission on Christmas Day. It was a late afternoon flight over North Vietnam. When I was dropping my bombs, I thought about what Ho Chi Minh had said earlier in response to a cease fire discussion: "If you will quit flying your warplanes over our country, we will quit shooting them down." Since he was playing hardball, bombing him on Christmas Day seemed apropos. Returning to the carrier, I made a "pinky landing," which is logged as a night landing, but there is still enough daylight to have visual references, making it much easier and safer than a totally dark night landing.

One thing we had plenty of aboard the carrier was good food. On Christmas Day, everyone aboard took a break to open presents from home and enjoy a sumptuous dinner of turkey and dressing with all the trimmings. Prior to leaving for this cruise, motion pictures were taken of many of our dependents at Lemoore and shown for the first time that evening. As one of our squadron mates said, "It's the Academy Award winner of the year and will have a longer run than *Gone with the Wind*."

January 3, 1968, our squadron participated in a large strike against targets in the Haiphong area. One of our pilots, LCDR Edward Estes, flying aircraft #405, was shot down by a surface-to-air missile, which hit the aircraft and exploded right behind the cockpit, destroying the rest of the plane completely. The only thing left of the Skyhawk was the cockpit, with Ed still inside it. His wingman was calling out over the radio for him to "eject." Of course, there was no working radio left for Ed to hear this call. Shortly after the radio call, he did eject from the cockpit and came floating down into Haiphong, being captured immediately. He was a POW until March 14, 1973.

With clearing skies, I was flying two flights a day and flew my one hundredth mission on January 8th. I can tell you that I delivered two MK 81 bombs and four MK-82 bombs somewhere in North Vietnam, but I don't have the specifics. At this time during the war, I believe the air force pilots were restricted to only flying a hundred missions before they were sent home. The navy must have been a "little short of pilots" as we had no restrictions on the maximum number of missions we could fly.

On January 9, 1968, our air wing found itself over Thanh Hoa, North Vietnam. We were participating in an Alpha strike against the Thanh Hoa Transshipment Complex. I was awarded the **Navy Achievement Medal** for my participation in the raid. The following citation describes what happened on that Alpha strike.

Citation
*The Secretary of the Navy takes pleasure in presenting the **Navy Achievement Medal** to LTJG Julian Harper, USNR.*

For meritorious achievement as a pilot of jet aircraft while attached to Attack Squadron One Hundred Twelve embarked on USS Kitty Hawk (CVA-63). On 9 January 1968, LTJG Harper was element leader of the A-4 Iron Hand element during a major air wing coordinated strike on the Thanh Hoa Transshipment Complex. He planned, coordinated, and skillfully executed the Iron Hand attack in such a manner as to provide the maximum protection to the main strike group. Finding no surface-to-air missile activity in the target area, he electronically acquired an enemy anti-aircraft artillery radar site. Correlating the display of his highly complex weapons system with visual estimates of the probable target location, he fired his missile which impacted on a known radar site that posed an immediate threat to the strike group and was followed immediately by a large, secondary explosion. LTJG Harper's skill and determination in the face of grave personal danger reflected great credit upon himself and were in keeping with the highest traditions of the naval service. LTJG Harper is authorized to wear the Combat "V."

Signed for the Secretary W. F. Bringle, Vice Admiral, US Navy.

Unfortunately, the weather took another turn for the worst in the skies over the North. There were a lot of clouds, rain, and haze that restricted our visibilities and kept us from striking important targets. Even with the poor visibility, by the middle of January, 1968, it was becoming apparent that the Communists were massing for a major attack against the South. Troop carriers, tanks, and other heavy equipment were being moved into position by the enemy, and these became targets for our Bronco pilots.

Khe Sanh was a marine base garrison located in northwest South Vietnam, close to the Laotian border and south of the DMZ. On January 21, 1968, the North Vietnamese began a heavy bombardment on the marines at that base. Because it was such an intense and prolonged attack, our government thought it was going to be like the battle for Dien Bien Phu, defended by the French in 1954. The decision was made to defend the base at all costs. This decision was going to cost the lives of about ten thousand North Vietnamese troops and five hundred US Marines. Our air wing took part in this huge defensive effort.

History would show that the battle for Khe Sanh was nothing like the battle for Dien Bien Phu because our resources were much better militarily. In some military circles, it was thought that this battle was just a diversion for the TET Offensive, which began on January 31, 1968.

Towards the end of January, the weather cleared in the North long enough for us to send an Alpha strike into the Vinh airfield. Pictures after the raid showed damage to the runways and surrounding area. We also conducted armed road reconnaissance sorties and found plenty of new trucks carrying supplies south. In the back of all of our minds, we knew we were helping the marines down south by hitting the enemy hard!

As mentioned earlier, during the TET cease fire of 1967, all of our forces honored an informal truce to respect the country's lunar New Year. The North Vietnamese took advantage of the situation to position men and equipment in the South. This was just a small pre-cursor to what they did during TET in 1968.

General VO Nguyen Giap, the leader of the People's Army of Vietnam (PAVN), planned an offensive that would strike many towns and cities at about the same time. He believed this surprise attack would weaken the resolve of the American people and also promote rebellion among the South Vietnamese population.

During the attacks in this time period, our squadron forced whole units into the open with our accurate bombing and strafing, inflicting heavy casualties upon the enemy. Many of our missions were flown at night, and most pilots saw heavy ground fire coming up at them, appearing as bright red basketballs.

Operation Arc Light was the code name our B-52 bombers used in the Vietnam War. Because of the huge advance of troops towards Khe Sanh, our little A-4s flew the same bombing tracks that the huge B-52s flew and were often in the area together. Not everything was coordinated between the services as it should have been. On one of my missions to bomb the enemy troops around Khe Sanh, I found my division not only in the same area as the B-52s, but directly beneath them. I knew this when I saw bombs falling all around us and looked up to see those gigantic aircraft empting their loads of bombs. Not thinking about how this could possibly happen, we all quickly turned our aircraft away from the falling bombs and, luckily, escaped without further incident. The B-52 attacks by the Seventh Air Force were just another work day for them. During the seventy-seven-day siege of Khe Sanh, they delivered their share of the hundred thousand tons of bombs that were dropped. To keep the base from being overrun by the North Vietnamese, they needed to be supplemented by additional aircraft types from both the air force and the navy.

We flew two different types of missions to help defend Khe Sanh. The first type was the Arc Light missions that were flown both day and night by our squadron, along with the rest of our carrier's air wing. A typical Arc Light mission started in the ready room with our normal brief, which included the different frequencies we would need to contact the ground control detachment at Khe Sanh. This detachment provided the controllers for our bombing attacks. We would fly these missions between fifteen thousand to twenty thousand feet. Normally, we flew down to South Vietnam in our four-plane division formation, carrying either two hundred and fifty- or five hundred-pound bombs.

The controller in Khe Sanh had access to all the different types of aircraft that he would be working with. This access included the trajectory of the weapons that were being delivered by the particular aircraft type against the enemy. For example, he would determine the exact time to tell the aircraft he was working with when to pickle (drop the bombs) by a computer-generated mark on his radar scope. There wasn't much distance between the base and the enemy in the Khe Sanh region, and the bombs were landing right in the area that was known to be occupied by the PAVN. To my knowledge, none of the bombs dropped by the air force or the navy ever landed off course onto the base, which speaks highly of the radar controllers.

The enemy troops were spending a lot of the nighttime in their tunnels, which had been dug prior to their attacks on the base. At night our bombs were set to delay detonation until after they hit the ground, which would cause damage to the tunnels. Our nightly bombing raids hopefully kept them awake by causing sand or dirt to fall from the tops of the tunnels down to where they were trying to sleep—if it didn't destroy the tunnels altogether.

From the altitude we were dropping our bombs, it was impossible to see the damage results. One night, I asked the controller if we were doing any good dropping our bombs down there. His response was, "If it weren't for all of you guys, the enemy would have overrun us long ago." In the daytime, still bombing from high altitude, we would have the bombs armed or set to explode right on impact with the ground, thus killing troops. After one of our bombing raids, a forward air controller working the Khe Sanh region visually identified large numbers of dead troops. These troops were in the area the radar controller had been informed about earlier, and his instructions lead to our direct hits.

The other type of missions we flew in Khe Sanh was low-altitude-release napalm bomb attacks. Napalm bombs are filled with a gel-type substance that spreads over an area and ignites on impact with the ground. They are designed to kill by burning, and in some cases, because of the intense fire, troops died by suffocating from the lack of oxygen caused from the flames. I remember seeing the famous picture of the young girl caught in a napalm bomb attack in South Vietnam—not related to the Khe Sanh region. That image, projected to the American people, showed the destructive power of this particular weapon and was offensive to a great many Americans. The Americans that it was not offensive to were our troops trying to keep the Khe Sanh base from being overrun by the well-equipped North Vietnamese regular troops.

Our Skyhawk flight division would each carry two napalm bombs to the Khe Sanh area. The delivery technique was to enter a shallow dive at a high rate of speed, usually between five hundred to five hundred and sixty knots, dropping the napalm bombs individually with a four-second interval at an altitude of five hundred feet. This allowed the gel with the fire ball to spread down the line of troops, keeping them from advancing. The planes would be separated by thirty seconds, enough time to let the blast from the bombs of the preceding aircraft dissipate so you would not be caught up in their fire balls. Our four aircraft would release a total of eight napalm bombs, covering a long distance.

As you can imagine, operating in a combat environment and performing these exact calculations required a great deal of skill. You can also imagine the enemy troops on the ground who were watching your flight of four roll in one at a time to deliver these bombs at such a low altitude. After the first plane attacked, they knew the exact route the next plane would take to deliver its bombs and would, therefore, be firing every weapon they had at that attacking aircraft. These attacks we made against the North Vietnamese soldiers were designated "close air support missions," which meant we were protecting our own troops from an advancing army, and it was extremely hazardous to the attacking aircraft. We were running down a line at five hundred feet, being fired at by an army of well-equipped soldiers (as opposed to the bomb runs we made over North Vietnam in which we would pull out of the attacks at a minimum of three thousand feet).

On one of my numerous missions to Khe Sanh, I returned to the carrier, and upon leaving the aircraft, my plane captain came after me and brought me back to the jet. He called my attention to the top of the ejection seat. I looked at the area where he was pointing, and approximately ten inches directly behind where my head would normally be, I saw a small-caliber bullet lodged into the frame of the ejection seat. Apparently, a North Vietnamese regular troop came very close to killing me and destroying the aircraft. Considering the speed of the plane at the time of the attack, ten inches one way or the other would have been very possible. Chalk it up to another lucky day for me!

After dropping my bombs on the enemy at Khe Sanh on the first day of February, I was going feet wet south of the DMZ. It was a clear day, and as I looked up ahead of my aircraft, I saw an island officially named Hon Co, but it was known to all of our pilots as Tigre Island (North Vietnamese spelling for Tiger Island). It had an elevation of 230 feet, and because it was only inhabited by enemy troops, we dropped our bombs there that were not used over South Vietnam due to poor weather conditions or any other reasons. As mentioned previously, we could not bring live ordnance back aboard the ship. The job of the troops on Tiger Island was to shoot at any US planes flying over their island. They didn't have much success at hitting them because our planes were flying too high.

I thought back to my first cruise in 1967 when I was returning to the ship and needed to get rid of a load of MK 81 (two hundred and fifty pound) bombs. It was during the first twenty-five sorties I had flown, and I was still learning the ropes about the combat configuration of the A-4 and how it changed its aerodynamics or flying characteristics. As I approached Tiger Island at twenty thousand feet, I rolled into our standard forty-five-degree dive run, which we normally started at eight thousand feet. At twenty thousand feet, with a full load of bombs, the Skyhawk was very heavy. As soon as I was established in this steep dive, I realized I had made a big mistake. I tried several times pulling back on the control stick to shallow out the dive. Each time, the only thing that happened was the airplane shook violently. At the altitude I was descending through, the air was very thin, making control of the aircraft almost impossible. The bombs were released at twelve thousand feet, but I was still unable to pull out of the dive. At about nine thousand feet, I began to regain control of the jet. Passing through seven thousand feet, I noticed I was being shot at by anti-aircraft guns that were located on the island. It was not just a few bullets; it was heavily concentrated cannon fire. At fifty-five hundred feet, I finally got the A-4 to begin a rapid climb back to a higher altitude and away from Tiger Island.

I had been flying alone during this maneuver since my wingman had safely dumped his bombs earlier, using a shallow dive, and was headed back to the ship. Meanwhile, I was putting on my air show for the enemy troops on the island, and had their cannon fire hit me, I would have been listed MIA.

I was flying sortie number 123 on February 1, 1968, when I thought back to that Tiger Island episode. Flying back over the safety of the sea, I continued thinking about combat flying.

The first cruise had taught me many valuable lessons. The first lesson was to plan to come back tomorrow and continue bombing the enemy as none of our targets were worth losing our lives over. The second lesson, which helped lesson number one, was never to make more than one run on your target. When you drop bombs, shoot guns, or launch missiles at your enemy, it really gets their attention. Once you have pulled up off the target and are heading back to feet wet, the enemy would really like to get another chance at shooting you out of the sky. If you were to make another run, it would give them that opportunity.

Mission planning, attention to detail, combat experience, and just plain dedication to destroying the targets assigned to me were becoming the standard I found myself caught up in during this time of my life. I realized that I had more expertise flying combat missions than most Americans had the opportunity to experience. I had become extremely good at destroying enemy targets, troops, and anything else I had been assigned to take out. In the true sense, I was becoming a modern day warrior.

The battle for Khe Sanh was raging daily and required our ship to remain on Yankee Station for an indefinite amount of time. Most of our missions were in support of the marines in Khe Sanh, but we also flew missions against targets located in North Vietnam.

Early in February, I was on a sortie at Khe Sanh when a forward air controller (FAC) came over the radio saying his plane had been hit. In 1968, the FACs were flying a push-pull twin engine Cessna O-2 Skymaster aircraft, which had replaced the old Cessna O-1 Birddog.

It turned out we were flying about five thousand feet directly above him when we received his stressful radio call. Stressful is a nice way to say he was crying and saying his plane had taken several hits. The most serious was a hit in the left wing strut, which holds the wing on the airplane. The weather was perfectly clear, and I could see that he was only two miles from the airfield located at Khe Sanh. Trying to calm him down, I transmitted a radio call saying he was very close to the field and should be on the ground in just a couple of minutes. Before he could answer, the strut broke, causing the left wing to fall off the aircraft. The Skymaster went spinning uncontrollably into the ground. I was dumbfounded and could not believe what I had just witnessed. I called the tower at the marine base and told them what had happened and the location of the crashed plane. My wingman and I continued on to our target, dropped our bombs, and returned to the ship in somewhat of a state of shock.

Chapter 17
CAPTAIN THOMAS HUDNER'S SEA STORY

C aptain Thomas Hudner was the executive officer on the Kitty Hawk during our second cruise. One night in the junior officers' bunkroom, we had a small get together, and Captain Hudner was one of attendees. The subject of awards or medals came up as many of us were receiving them. It turned out the captain, who was a LTJG at the time of the award, was one of eleven men who had received the **Congressional Medal of Honor** during the Battle of Chosen Reservoir. He was the only naval aviator to receive the **Medal of Honor** in the Korean War. We asked him to tell us what he did to be awarded the nation's highest medal. Most of us agreed that it wasn't a medal we wanted because it was usually presented to the wife posthumously. It's been almost fifty years, but this is his description of the events that happened as I remember him telling our spellbound group of aviators.

He was a pilot in Fighter Squadron 32 aboard the aircraft carrier USS Leyte, flying the F-4U Corsair. The Corsair was a powerful, gull-wing navy fighter plane used in World War II and the Korean War. On December 4, 1950, he flew the mission for which he was awarded the **Congressional Medal of Honor**. He was trying to save his wingman's life during the battle of Chosen Reservoir.

His wingman, Ensign Jesse L. Brown, the navy's first black naval aviator, had received a hit in his wing by the Chinese troops and was losing fuel at an alarming rate. He was unable to make it back out to sea and had to crash-land on the side of a mountain. At that time in aviation history, the pilots preferred to stay with the plane during the crash-landing instead of bailing out. LTJG Hudner watched Jesse crash-land his Corsair and observed there was a small fire on the airplane, but Jesse was not getting out of the cockpit.

Tom called the carrier on his radio and told them he was going to try to land beside Jesse and attempt to pull him out of the cockpit. He requested the ship send the rescue helicopter in to pick up both of them. After some discussion with the carrier, he landed his plane beside Jesse's aircraft.

Tom was slightly injured in his landing but managed to run over to pull Jesse out of the cockpit. He said Jesse was losing a lot of blood and was barely conscious. His leg was pinned in such a way that Tom could not free him. Shortly after he tried, unsuccessfully, to put out the small fire by using handfuls of snow, the ship's helicopter arrived. Several of the crew continued to try to put out the fire and tried using a crash axe to free Jesse but to no avail. Jesse asked them to amputate his leg so he could get out of the cockpit. No one thought that was a good idea as they had no equipment to perform such an act. As night was approaching, they had to leave a barely conscious Jesse in the cockpit to return to the carrier.

Due to poor weather conditions that delayed further rescue attempts, on December 7, 1950, a flight of Corsairs took off from the carrier. They carried Napalm bombs to destroy the plane and to keep Jesse's body from being taken by the North Koreans. All the pilots were members of squadron 32 and friends of Jesse. When they arrived over the crash site, they could see that some of Jesse's clothes had been removed and he was obviously dead. The flight then proceeded to drop Napalm bombs on the plane, incinerating the crash site along with Jesse's body.

For Hudner's heroic action, President Truman awarded him the **Congressional Medal of Honor** on April 13, 1951.

On the subject of rescue missions, I would like to touch on a few rescue-type activities I was involved in with my squadron. As you can imagine, when the ship was launching a lot of aircraft on an Alpha strike, there was a high probability that one or more aircraft might be shot down. After the launch and, in some cases, after the recovery cycle are completed, more aircraft were brought up from the hanger bay to the flight deck to prepare for the next launch cycle. While this was occurring, the Alpha strike group would be approaching their targets.

At least one Skyhawk that came up from the hanger bay was designated to be a rescue aircraft. It was armed with either 2.75 rockets, five-inch Zuni rockets, or Gatling guns. All of these weapons were excellent to use in a rescue scenario. Typically, the rescue aircraft, known as the rescap aircraft, was parked behind the island and pulled up very close to the landing area behind the foul line. A foul line is a painted line on the flight deck that separates the landing area from the parking area.

One day I had rescap duty and was sitting there in my A-4, watching the recovery cycle. The last plane recovered was the A-3 Whale as it operated as a tanker for planes that might need some extra fuel. It was the second largest aircraft, which put it right behind the RA-5C in size to land on the carrier. When it came aboard, the plane's right wing seemed to pass extremely close to the nose of my A-4, and it landed close to the centerline of the landing area.

After my rescap duty cycle was over, I went down to the ready room and relayed what I had just experienced up on the flight deck to the skipper. You have to remember; we were operating in a war-time environment. The skipper listened to me and said, "Jules, if you are that afraid of being hit by the tanker, next time you have the duty, just get out of the plane until it has landed." As usual, I said, "Yes, sir!"

It wasn't long until I was assigned rescap duty again. I was sitting in my A-4, as was the normal procedure, with the cockpit canopy open in close to ninety-degree heat when the recovery cycle started. I thought to myself that since I had made such a scene talking to the skipper previously, I would follow his advice and get out of the plane. I walked over behind the carrier's island and watched the planes returning from their missions. As the A-3 Whale was approaching, I noticed he was having a little trouble lining up with the carrier's flight deck. When he touched down on the carrier deck, he was right of the landing centerline. It all happened very fast, as did everything in a jet. His right wing passed over the foul line and through the first three feet of my aircraft's nose. Besides damage to the nose of the aircraft, numerous aircraft components were destroyed. Had I been sitting in the aircraft, it would have been a close call.

I went down to the ready room and found the skipper reading the message log book. I approached him and asked, "Did you see what just happened on the flight deck?" He replied, "Yes, I saw it on the PLATT. From now on, while standing rescap duty, we will all get out of the aircraft during the recovery cycle." I answered him as usual, "Yes, sir," but I was thinking it was nice for my concerns to be validated.

Chapter 18
ROAD RECONNAISSANCE MISSION; LIBERTY; NAVY DETAILER

O
n February 9, 1968, I was teamed up with our soft-spoken operations officer, Joe Eichinger, to conduct a night road reconnaissance mission over North Vietnam near the Thanh Hoa area. Joe and I had flown together frequently, due to my lack of seniority on our first cruise. It was normal for the senior pilots to fly with the more junior pilots in our squadron. With the new arrival of additional aviators in the squadron during our second cruise, I found myself in a much more senior position and, as a result, flew less with Joe, the third-most senior pilot in the squadron.

As we briefed the mission together, we were concerned with the usual SAM threats. It was decided we would coast into North Vietnam, just north of Thanh Hoa, at an altitude of eight thousand feet, which was low enough to evade some of the SAM threats that we knew were located farther to the north. We were each carrying six MK-81 (two hundred and fifty-pound bombs), which were great to use against trucks because you could carry more of them, and each one was plenty big enough to destroy the target. Because of the darkness, we were going to use our tacan instruments in the air-to-air mode. This would tell each of us how far apart we were from each other in miles. Joe would maintain the eight thousand-foot level of altitude, and I would climb up to nine thousand feet. Because we would not be using our navigational lights, this would insure that we would not collide with each other if we crossed paths during our hunt for cars and trucks. It is important to remember that we very seldom flew a straight line as we would be an easier target for the gunners on the ground to hit. We would go up and down, side to side, or jinxing, as we called it. The two of us would maintain a basic heading and stay within five miles of each other, talking very little on the radio.

It all sounded perfectly planned, but as usual in combat, some things do not go according to the plans. As we hit feet dry, Joe turned to the left as we had briefed it, and I turned a little to the right. It was a beautiful evening, with a full moon providing great visibility. I am embarrassed to say I only made one little mistake; I forgot to climb to nine thousand feet.

After about five to ten minutes of searching for targets, I looked over to the left of my aircraft and suddenly saw Joe's aircraft rapidly approaching me through the night air at the same altitude. Apparently, he saw me at the same time because we both began a rapid turn in the opposite direction, and the last thing I saw was Joe's aircraft wing go into the vertical position, indicating he was pulling g's as hard as I was. We pulled about six g's to keep from running into each other. I don't know how close we came to a mid-air collision, maybe a hundred yards or ten feet, but I know it was extremely close. Attention to detail again raised its ugly head; I forgot to climb and almost cost the loss of two combat aircraft, including their pilots, one of which was me.

Joe came on the radio and asked me to climb to the pre-briefed altitude. We continued our hunt for targets and finally found several trucks. Joe's bombs fell right on them, but mine missed by a hundred yards or so, probably due to my "upsetting" screw up. Arriving back at the carrier, we debriefed the mission, which was standard practice. We discussed in a calm, normal manner what had caused the problem, and nothing else was ever said about it. To this day, it was one of the most embarrassing and dangerous things that ever happened to me while flying an airplane.

The last day of our first line period was on February 21, 1968. My flight assignment on that day was to conduct another road reconnaissance mission or "road recce" as we called it; this meant my wingman and I would split up and cover as much of the highway as we could, while staying within about ten miles of each other. We were looking for cars, trucks, and basically anything that could be used to move war materials down to the South. During our brief, we had agreed to operate between the Vinh and Thanh Hoa area. We would concentrate on Route One, the major highway that ran north and south.

As our planes approached the coast, we split up, with my wingman going south as I proceeded north. Route 1 was easy to find as it wasn't very far inland and paralleled the coast. I had only gone a few miles when I spotted a truck heading south. As I positioned my aircraft for the attack, I called my wingman on the radio and told him what I had found. He came back on the air and said he would continue to look as he hadn't seen anything yet.

My plane was loaded with four, five hundred-pound MK 82 bombs, plus sixty rounds of 20mm cannon bullets for its pair of machine guns. Positioning the Skyhawk for the attack required me to descend rapidly to about three thousand feet and then begin a shallow, ten-degree dive run in the direction of the target.

The truck driver had no idea what was about to happen to him as he continued driving down the highway. My speed increased in the descent to about five hundred knots, and I began firing the machine guns at fifteen hundred feet. As I continued to fire on the target, I could see my bullets hitting the truck; pieces of it were flying in all directions. As I had mentioned earlier, things happen fast in a jet. I kept expecting to see the target burst into flames, but it didn't. I finally pulled out of the dive run at the low altitude of three hundred feet, suffering from a small case of target fixation, and began a steep climb back up to eight thousand feet. Target fixation occurs when you concentrate so hard on the target that you forget to fly the airplane. This has been known to cause pilots to crash.

Once I got the nose heading upward, I looked in my rear view mirrors and saw that the truck had come to a complete stop, and the driver had stepped outside the cab of his truck. He was looking up at my airplane with his arm at a ninety-degree angle, and I could see that he was giving me the universal symbol meaning, "Stick it where the sun don't shine."

While my mind was processing this symbol, I was thinking about all the times I had seen similar symbols directed at me while I had been driving a car back home. Without much thought or hesitation, I leaned forward and armed the four, five hundred-pound bombs. Reaching eight thousand feet and positioning myself for the attack, I rolled in on the truck. At fifty-six hundred feet, I released the bombs in a straight line down Route 1, which acted as a lead-in arrow to the target. The bombs were set to release one right after another from the aircraft so that they landed approximately fifty feet apart when they struck the ground. Landing right on target, they completely destroyed the truck and significantly damaged Route 1.

As you can imagine, we were involved in a war where the North Vietnamese called us air pirates and never applied the Geneva

Convention rules to us when we were captured. The record showed that during captivity our pilots were tortured and sometimes killed. Our flying missions were designed to destroy equipment that was moving weapons down to South Vietnam to be used against our American and South Vietnamese troops. Unfortunately, many of the enemy troops driving these vehicles were also killed. War is brutal and nasty.

This was one mission that I felt personally involved in since I had the unusual experience of personal contact with the enemy. There was no doubt in my mind that after all the training I had accomplished, combined with each combat mission completed, including today's 138th combat sortie, I had, indeed, become a flying warrior. From that point forward, I no longer worried about getting shot down or captured. If my number was up, so be it. I realized that I, along with all the other pilots in our squadron, was the best in the history of our country at doing this particular job. Not only did we have the skills and ability to destroy our approved targets, but we also did it with a professional attitude that made the navy proud.

The following is an article I assisted our skipper in writing on February 20, 1968; it was published in our *Bronco Bulletin*:

Dear Broncos,
The first combat period of this cruise is still underway. After more than sixty days of sustained effort, with fewer men and airplanes, we have flown more hours and combat missions than during any similar period on the last cruise. Our missions have ranged from strikes into the enemy's heartland cities, Hanoi and Haiphong, to direct support of our Marines and soldiers on the ground in Khe Sanh, South Vietnam. We have struck at trains in daylight and trucks loaded with supplies at night. Ammunition dumps, SAM sites, and anti-aircraft emplacements have felt the kick of the Broncos. We used all the weapons in our arsenal which the A-4

can carry. Our pilots have used these weapons with deadly skill in order to aid those of our countrymen and our allies who are at close grips with the North Vietnamese soldier. We are accomplishing our purpose.

This effort is being accomplished through the determination of all hands. The work of the men who are maintaining our aircraft, loading the ordnance, and taking care of the administrative details of the squadron is outstanding. Despite long and irregular hours, our men have done all, and more, than has been asked of them, but it appears that our enemies are determined to give us little rest.

I am proud to work with a group of men who are so able and willing to do what is needed since you know that they are carrying out a vital portion of our country's defense.

On February 22nd, we found ourselves steaming to Cubi Point to enjoy some much-needed rest and relaxation after just completing a **record sixty-one days of combat duty** on the line. The rumor that reached our pilots from Rear Admiral Don Rush, Commander, Task Force Seventy-Seven, was as follows: "Unless my pilots kill somebody in Cubi, leave them alone."

As usual, when we were berthed at Cubi, you could find most of our air wing pilots at the officers' club. The old officers' club, where we had enjoyed the dead bat game, had been bulldozed to a flat piece of land and a new club had been built up on top of a hill overlooking the bay. It was a beautiful split-level design. When you walked through the front doors, you were immediately looking at several slot machines, where I personally deposited many quarters, hoping to hit the big jackpot. Unfortunately, the big jackpot alluded me, but I did hit enough cherries and sevens to keep me solvent!

Walking pass these machines, you found yourself in a huge dining and dancing area that was spectacular. It was designed to accommodate a large number of base personnel, complete, most nights, with a band so the base couples could enjoy dancing. Gone were the overhead rafters, so playing dead bat was out of the question. The entire room was elegant and looked very sophisticated.

On the west side of the room were carpeted, large steps that went up to the second level, approximately eight feet above the dance floor. When you reached the top of the steps, you were looking at a beautiful bar that was at least one hundred feet long, overlooked the bay, and was staffed by numerous bartenders in the evenings. This area could hold several hundred patrons and is where the pilots spent most of their time in the club.

It was in this setting, on an earlier in-port period, one of our air wing pilots had ordered a hundred stingers. At twenty-five cents apiece, the total bill came to twenty-five dollars. At the time, we all agreed that this was a cool thing to do. Unfortunately, during our last line period, the pilot who had ordered the hundred stingers had been shot down and was MIA. One night, after a few drinks in honor of him, one of our pilots ordered twelve hundred stingers. I thought all the bartenders were going to go crazy! We all chipped in the money required to pay for the drinks, which amounted to three hundred dollars. It took a while, but the air wing aviators drank all the stingers.

By now you can imagine we all knew each other pretty well, and after all those drinks, we began to look for something else to do instead of listening to all the same stories over again. The game that was devised was playing aircraft carrier.

It was around nine o'clock when we began to play this new game. The club was full of base personnel, including wives. They were all on the lower level, dancing and having a quiet, enjoyable evening.

Meanwhile, the pilots had discovered that the large chairs in the bar had rollers on the bottom of the legs. In the intoxicated state that we were in, it was decided that we could make these chairs fly like an airplane. Pretending to be on an aircraft carrier, the flight deck officer positioned the chair (with a pilot in its seat) approximately ten feet from the top step that led down to the dance floor. Four other pilots, who wanted to be part of this fun, new game, came forward to act as the catapult system. Two of them positioned themselves on each side of the newly devised airplane and held the pilot flying this machine by each of his arms to act like a sling shot. Another pilot appeared and acted as the catapult officer. He stepped in front and to the side of the pilot and his "plane." He began to give the turn-up signal by taking his right hand, holding it over his head, and making fast circular motions. This was the signal for the pilot to check that his engine was at 100 percent power and all was ready to launch. Remember, you have to salute the catapult officer before he will give the signal to launch the plane. It was decided that raising the right leg would take the place of a hand salute since his arms were being held by four other pilots.

The band downstairs was playing "Somewhere My Love," as I remember. Many base personnel couples were dancing close together, having a good time. In this setting, the catapult officer, having received the raised-leg salute, gave the launch signal to the four pilots acting as the catapult system. The chair/airplane began to accelerate down the carpet, heading towards the top of the stairs, while all the air wing took time out from drinking to watch this launch. Reaching the end of the carpeted second floor, the newly created airplane did begin to fly. It flew quite well until it was pulled down to the first level by gravity. Apparently, the pilots forgot to build wings on the plane, a simple mistake.

It struck the dance floor with a resounding "thud" and began its arrested landing by running over the dancers who had been unaware of what was happening. By the time the pilot flying his plane had come to a total arrested landing, numerous husbands and wives lay on the landing/dance floor area. Amazingly, no one was seriously hurt.

The air wing pilots at the bar began laughing hysterically, which really irritated the base personnel and their wives on the dance floor. The base officer of the day (OOD) was called, and while he was "chewing out" the air wing, Fighter Squadron 213, the Black Lions, dispatched several of its pilots, along with other squadron volunteers, outside to find the OOD's truck. Obviously, thievery was not a major problem on the base as the truck was found unlocked. Numerous pilots apparently pushed the truck in an attempt to get it started, but, unfortunately, it wound up going over a cliff at the end of the road. Failing in this mission, the pilots returned to the bar and continued drinking.

By this time, which was a little past ten, the captain of the base appeared in a furious state. He was the same captain who had, a year earlier, ended our dead bat game at the old officers' club by making us come down from the rafters. It took him a while to wade through the base personnel on the dance floor to reach our group. I don't recall much of what he said, but I remember the club was closed, and most of us wound up walking in some form of lose formation down the hill, arriving at the carrier. It must have been the war environment we were operating in, but we never heard anything else about the night we ordered and drank the twelve hundred stingers.

The navy detailer is the individual responsible for interviewing and helping the naval officer decide what type of duty station would best fit the navy and his needs after he leaves his current position. My detailer arrived during our second cruise and interviewed me. I had already received the official navy letter offering me a **regular navy commission** instead of my reserve commission. I was trying to decide whether to accept it or not.

One of the questions I asked the detailer was how combat officers fair in advancing up the military chain of command, making higher rank as compared with non-combat officers. The answer was very interesting. He told me, "Jules, the truth is that the non-combat officer will typically advance faster than the combat officer. This is because while you have been out here fighting a war, he has been back in the states greasing the rails for advancement. As you know, you guys don't take any sh-t from anyone, and this does not normally help you in the advancement cycle. Of course, there are exceptions to this rule. In your case, with your outgoing personality, public affairs experience, and combat skill under your belt, you could apply to be a Blue Angel or go to Monterey to finish college."

I thought about all the fine naval aviators I had known who had been killed in combat and in peacetime operations. Carrier duty is extremely hazardous in the best of situations, and you don't have those situations all the time.

At this time, the airlines were hiring as many military pilots as they could to fill the vacating captain seats on their carriers. The pay was much better than the navy, and there were no seven-to eight- month deployments away from home. With a child on the way, thoughts of family weighed heavily on my decision process.

After having an enjoyable talk with the detailer, I told him I would think it over, consult with my wife, and let him know what I decided to do.

Chapter 19
SECOND LINE PERIOD; YOKOSUKA, JAPAN

Leaving the Philippines on the second of March, we steamed back towards Yankee Station. Once again, we were limited by bad weather and forced to divert from strikes in the north to areas farther south where the skies were clear.

I flew two missions on March 4th and two missions on March 5th. On March 6th, I led a section of two A-4s away from the battlefields of Vietnam and crossed several hundred miles of open ocean to deliver them to the Sangley Point Naval Air Station. This air station, surrounded by Manila Bay, was about eight miles southwest of Manila in the Philippines.

After leaving the carrier, my wingman and I climbed up to altitude and met up with the A-3 tanker. We filled up our tanks with jet fuel and continued on towards the Philippines. When you are flying above thirty thousand feet and looking down at the ocean, you can't help but think,

I hope this airplane's engine doesn't quit. We began to paint (see on radar) the Island of Luzon at a range of two hundred miles. Descending down to an altitude of two hundred feet, our A-4s passed a few fishing boats. Arriving at the shoreline, we adjusted our course and flew parallel to it, enjoying the beach view.

It was a very relaxing flight, and while approaching our destination, the Taal Volcano, which was erupting, came into view. I had never seen anything like it before. The volcano was located on an island in a lake that was on an island. It's located approximately thirty-one miles from Manila, the capital of the Philippines. As we got nearer to the volcano, which had begun its eruption on January 31, 1968, I had the urge to fly through it. The eruptions were still significant as fire, smoke, and pieces of molten rock were being tossed upward into the sky.

At twenty-four years of age, having completed 142 combat missions, and expecting the birth of my first child in two months, I made the decision to act on my instincts. I informed my wingman of my decision to fly through it, and he said he would move over and watch from a distance. I slowed the aircraft speed down from three hundred and fifty knots to two hundred and fifty knots, in case I needed to eject in the event I hit a rock from the erupting volcano. Looking back at this decision, I see it made absolutely no sense and would have been considered "stupid" by any logical mind. The only way I can even remotely justify it was that I felt indestructible. Obviously, I had been exposed to "way too much combat time."

I must say that as I entered the eruption area, I felt a thrill, and that thrill increased as I saw molten rocks come flying past me in an upward direction. Remember, things happen fast in a jet. I was through it in a manner of seconds and emerged on the other side, unscathed.

Arriving in Sangley Point, I climbed down from the cockpit of the Skyhawk, took the beer that was handed to me by the plane captain, and did a visual inspection of the airplane. There was no damage done to it at all. To the best of my knowledge, I am probably the only person to have ever flown through an erupting volcano and lived to tell about it. Once again, in a single-seat aircraft, nothing is known by anyone else except your wingman. Had the navy found out about this event or had the aircraft been damaged, it is unknown what form of discipline might have been considered. In war time, many events simply slip through the cracks as this one did.

On March 12th, the weather cleared over North Vietnam, and our Bronco pilots took part in a coordinated strike against Haiphong. Flying through heavy flak and surface-to-air missiles, our pilots nevertheless got through and struck bridges within the city limits, placing their ordnance right on target. Photographs taken minutes after the strike showed heavy damage to the bridges.

On March 21, 1968, I had flown a night sortie and wrote an article for our *Bronco Bulletin* about that particular flight. The sortie was briefed to be a "standard" night road reconnaissance mission. The primary mission of the flight was to locate and destroy enemy trucks strategic to the movement of enemy men and material to the South. The secondary mission, if no trucks could be found, was to bomb a supply storage area located at the end of the road reconnaissance flight. The trick was to find the trucks with their lights on and bomb them before they heard you and turned them off. The truck drivers in North Vietnam were pretty proficient at hearing airplanes and quite often secured their lights when we were still several miles away. Once the lights went out, it was necessary to drop flares overhead to illuminate the area.

A nighttime dive-bombing run was a very exciting adventure. It was done almost entirely on instruments, and the only time you looked out of the cockpit was to put the target in the gun-sight piper. As the airplane approached the correct altitude for releasing the bombs, the pilot pressed the bomb pickle switch and then started a hard pull back on the stick to gain a higher altitude. The whole run took less than forty seconds, but each one was different. Flak or surface-to-air missiles often created additional hazards, besides those normally associated with night bombing. Flak appeared as bright red basketballs, and since your depth perception was limited at night, it was impossible to tell exactly how far away the bursts were. To complicate the problem of the ground gunners seeing us, we kept all of our navigation lights turned off when we flew over the beach at night. This required each aircraft to maintain altitude separation from each other so the possibility of having a mid-air collision would be avoided.

We coasted in south of Vinh and proceeded by our pre-briefed route into the supply storage area. The sun had just set as we crossed the coast and visibility was diminishing rapidly. This was the worst time of the day to fly into combat. From the air, it was hard to see anything on the ground, but from the ground, an airplane stood out against the sky. Adjusting myself to the instruments, I flew at my assigned altitude. My wingman called out he had just dropped his flares. Half a minute later, they lit off several thousand feet above the ground. I made a pass over the top of them and spotted the storage area on the ground. Calling this out to my wingman, I commenced a climb to the left, and we set up our bombing pattern. We planned to make several runs, which we normally didn't do in the daytime, but because we were much harder to see at night, we thought it was an acceptable risk to take.

Dropping several bombs at a time, we corrected for wind drift from each other's hits, and on my final run, my last two hundred and fifty-pound bomb struck squarely in the center of the target. Flames leaped skyward. To gain a better view, I pulled off the target to the right instead of the left. Off my port wing, I noticed tracers flying by where I would have been. It appeared to be the Shilka, a 23mm Russian anti-aircraft gun named after a river in Russia, capable of firing four thousand rounds per minute. You could always tell that particular weapon as it looked like a garden hose spraying bullets all over the sky. We had sent somebody on the ground to general quarters, and they were really shooting at us. Had I pulled off to the left, as I had on my previous runs, the bullets would have been much closer to my aircraft. I began to maneuver the aircraft to make a harder target for the gunners to hit. While all this was going on in the air, a series of explosions were erupting on the ground. As we left the target area, it looked like a full square mile of the ground was on fire.

After the bombing runs, both aircraft departed enemy territory and affected a rendezvous over the silent waters of the Gulf. As I waited for my wingman to join up with me, my mind was wandering back in the past somewhere. I had engaged the aircraft autopilot, and I was just sitting in it like a relaxed passenger. I happened to glance up into my rear view mirrors, and for one startling, split second, I thought I was being followed by a police car. The inky blackness of night was being cut by a bright red, rotating beacon not twenty feet from my starboard wing. Unconsciously I glanced at my airspeed; I was going over three hundred mph! Suddenly, it dawned on me. The red light in my mirrors was the anti-collision light on my wingman's airplane—not a police car! We proceeded back to the ship and landed without further incident or a traffic ticket. Another night strike completed.

On March 25th and 26th, I flew two additional night sorties and completed mission number 160. Operating under the Arc Light missions, my squadron mates and I helped to keep the North Vietnamese from overrunning the Khe Sanh base in South Vietnam.

March 26th marked the end of our second line period, and we began the trip to Yokosuka, Japan. Slowly, the temperature began to drop, and on the first of April, we arrived in port. We were most fortunate to arrive at the height of the famed Japanese cherry blossom season. The magnificent trees provided endless opportunities for squadron amateur photography. Most of the five thousand men aboard the USS Kitty Hawk made a beeline for building A-33. This building housed foreign merchandise, stereo equipment, Japanese clothes, telescopes, and just about anything else you might want to buy, all at a tremendous cost savings. A-33 was larger than two gymnasiums put together, but the first day in port it was packed with sailors, not only from our ship but from destroyers and cruisers also in port. As most of our men could testify, it was a real shopping experience to try to buy something under those crowded conditions. We succeeded beautifully, however, and several people bought more merchandise than they could possibly carry back to the ship by themselves and had to ask their shipmates for a helping hand!

Tours, rest and relaxation, and shopping in "Thieves Alley" kept all of us busy until we left Yokosuka on April 8, 1968. While we were in Yokosuka, President Johnson announced over radio and television that bombing would be limited to the southern part of North Vietnam.

Chapter 20
THIRD LINE PERIOD; HO CHI MINH TRAIL; CHU LE HIGHWAY BRIDGE

Operating under President Johnson's new policy, we commenced flight operations on the morning of April 12, 1968. Most of our missions were flown down into South Vietnam due to bad weather up north. On April 15th, the weather began to break, and we flew many reconnaissance missions in the southern part of North Vietnam. Finding trucks, junks, and many bridges, our squadron pilots delivered their ordnance with deadly accuracy on the targets.

I had been assigned to a flight of four A-4s to go into North Vietnam just south of Thanh Hoa and destroy a bridge. We had just completed our bombing runs and noted that the bridge was completely gone when we received a Mayday distress call. One of our F-4 Phantom jets had been hit by ground fire and was trying to make it out to feet wet. The jet was just south of our position when we visually identified him. Our flight leader turned in the direction of the Phantom, and we followed him out to the Gulf of Tonkin. As we approached feet wet, the F-4 burst into flames, and the two crewmembers ejected. They were a little bit ahead of us, and when the parachutes opened, they drifted down into the water about a half of mile from the shore line. Both the pilot and the radar intercept officer (RIO) were able to rid themselves of their parachutes with all the tangling shroud lines and climb into their individual life rafts. We called for a rescue helicopter to come and pick up the aviators.

Shortly after the crew landed in the water, a shore artillery battery started firing at them. Our flight of four Skyhawks began a circular pattern designed for one of us to have the nose of our A-4 headed downward in an attack position, which was a standard procedure in a rescue operation. Each time we approached the firing shore battery, they stopped and ducked for cover. Unfortunately, my two 20mm machine guns jammed on the first pass, but I continued to fly the pattern with the other Skyhawks, keeping the North Vietnamese gunners seeking shelter. While flying the circular pattern, I had time to pull out my super 8 movie camera and film what was happening to the pilots in the water.

A rescue helicopter was approaching one of the downed pilots just as a cannon round exploded about a hundred yards short of the pilot and helicopter's position. The rescue team wasted no time lowering the cable down to the crewmember, which took about a minute. Just then, another cannon round landed about a hundred yards ahead of them both. The helicopter pilot knew the next round was going to be right on target, so he began to accelerate away from his position, dragging the recently attached Phantom crewmember along on top of the water.

Within thirty seconds, the third cannon round landed right where they had been, but fortunately, the sharp helicopter pilot had moved away from the danger area. The crewmember was loaded aboard the chopper, and it turned around to pick up the other downed airman.

We began to fly down low over the water between the shore battery and downed airmen to fire off chaff (material like aluminum foil) out the rear fuselage of our airplanes. We hoped if the guns were controlled by radar this would confuse the controller by jamming the radar signals. The other crewmember was picked up without much delay, and they were more than happy to be returned to their carrier. My movie camera picked up this entire sequence, and it was really amazing to watch.

Because of the nature of the rescue, the hazards involved, and the successful outcome of the rescue portion of the mission, I was awarded our country's **Air Medal**.

Citation

*The President of the United States takes pleasure in presenting the **Air Medal (Bronze Star in lieu of the First Award)** to Lieutenant Julian Harvey Harper, USNR.*

For heroic achievement in aerial flight as a pilot of jet aircraft while attached to Attack Squadron One Hundred Twelve embarked in USS KITTY HAWK (CVA-63). On 15 April 1968, Lieutenant Harper was a wingman for the On-Scene Commander during the successful rescue of two airmen downed perilously close to the coast of North Vietnam. He demonstrated daring airmanship, great courage and provided vital assistance in the rescue operation. He expertly maintained flight integrity in an extremely hazardous environment and provided vigilant lookout for this section. Though unable to fire his own cannon, and in spite of danger to himself, he repeatedly made feigned attacks to harass enemy shore batteries who had taken the downed airmen and rescue helicopter under continuous and withering fire. Lieutenant

*Harper's superb airmanship, great courage and devotion to duty
reflected great credit upon himself and were in keeping with the
highest traditions of the United States Naval Service.*

*For the President, W. F. Bringle, Vice Admiral, United
States Navy.*

The Ho Chi Minh trail was the American name given to the
route that ran from North Vietnam to South Vietnam. It was used
to carry weapons of all kinds, troops, and anything else the North
needed to further their war efforts in the South. The route was only
accessible from air strikes as the trail ran through the neutral countries
of Laos and Cambodia. Unfortunately for our airstrikes, the trail was
located in a huge rain forest and mostly covered by a triple-canopy
jungle. It had been used as a foot path for centuries to carry on trade
between different areas of the region. During our time in the Vietnam
area, 1966-1968, the North Vietnamese used animals, including
elephants and water buffalo, to move supplies south—besides using
fairly modern trucks that were supplied by Russia, China, and other
communist countries,

Any kind of a book about our air campaign in Vietnam would
not be complete without a discussion of the time, material, and lives
that were lost interdicting this logistical support route created by the
North Vietnamese. I personally flew up to 10 percent of my missions
expending all types of ordnance on this supply route.

A typical mission included arriving in South Vietnam and contacting
a forward air controller (FAC). As mentioned previously, the Ho Chi
Minh trail was so heavily covered by the forest, our high-speed jets were
unable to find truck convoys unless we were lucky enough to find them
out in the open, crossing streams or small rivers.

However, the FAC received daily briefings about movements and
locations of equipment on this supply route. When we hooked up with

him, he had located the convoys either moving south or stopped in a "truck park." The truck park was generally protected by both natural and man-made camouflage and sometimes shielded by hills and caves. After he described the area to us, he would fire a smoke-producing shell into the general target area. For his own protection, he might shoot the smoke rocket hundreds of yards away from the target. When we saw the smoke coming up through the dense forest, the FAC would tell us how far away from the target and in what direction from the smoke he wanted us to drop our bombs or fire our rockets.

The enemy troops always seemed to find a place to put an anti-aircraft machine gun site where they could see through the forest and shoot at us while we were in our dive runs. Over the years, many of our jets were shot down by these enemy troops riding along with the convoys.

On April 21, 1968, I was one of a flight of four Skyhawks sent to interdict a section of the Ho Chi Minh trail or destroy trucks if we could find them. I was the only plane in our division of four aircraft equipped with two of the AGM 12C, Bullpup missiles. The rest of the flights were loaded with the five-inch Zuni rockets.

The FAC notified us he had a convoy of trucks located in a truck park and wanted us to attack them. He was being held a good distance away due to a machine gun site that was actively shooting at him when he got within range of the target. The gun site was described to us as being on top of an exposed hill close to the truck convoy.

Approaching the area described to us, we easily found the anti-aircraft machine gun as it was firing at us. Fortunately, we were at a high enough altitude that the chances of hitting us were slim. Three of my wingmen broke away from me as I positioned my aircraft into a firing position. I descended down to an altitude of five thousand feet, and at a distance of about three miles from the machine gun site, I fired one of the Bullpup missiles that was loaded on my plane.

Steering the missile to the target, it exploded at a preset altitude of about fifty feet, sending exploding fragments all over the gun site and its operators. The site became quiet, and the three other A-4s fired their Zuni rockets into the foliage that the FAC directed them to hit. Because of heavy jungle in the Laos and Cambodia areas, we constantly joked about making match sticks out of the trees with the weapons we dropped on them.

The FAC told me there was a tunnel that the trucks used to arrive at the truck park. After he described its' location in detail to me, I fired my final Bullpup missile in the direction of his instructions. You have to understand, seeing anything under the jungle foliage was impossible from our position. Steering the missile to the general target area, I saw it penetrate the trees followed by a tremendous secondary explosion.

During this time period, the FACs were transmitting the results of the raids over our radio frequency. I guess they were required by headquarters to describe the results of all the missions being flown. As he descended directly over the burning target area at a low enough altitude and such a slow speed that I was concerned he might be shot down, he came over the radio and said in an excited voice, "You must have hit the truck fuel supply area." I had long since ignored their reports as I felt they were just guesses of what we had destroyed. I do recall what he reported to us on that particular day. We had destroyed one machine gun site, three trucks, a fuel supply area, and we had killed approximately forty enemy troops. I thought to myself, *At least we didn't kill any elephants* which were used in addition to trucks to move supplies south.

The next day, April 22nd, my roommate, Bob Saville, and I were sent out to bomb the Chu Le Highway Bridge, located in North Vietnam. I had been moved into a stateroom, which housed just two officers instead of the six housed in the junior officers' bunkroom. This move had occurred the first part of January when Bob's previous roommate,

Ed Estes, was shot down. His plane was destroyed over Haiphong, and Ed was taken as a prisoner of war.

The Chu Le Highway Bridge had been targeted many times by both the air force and navy pilots. I recalled reading on the ship that more than three hundred sorties had been flown against this bridge, and it was still intact. As you can imagine, bridges are hard to destroy because the construction techniques require them to be anchored in the ground by substantial buried pillars that support the structure.

This was to be mission number 168 for myself, and I was flying an A-4 with bureau number 148588. We were flying one mission a day but sometimes two. They all required an extensive brief to know where the enemy gun and missile batteries were located so you could avoid them. Each day, all of our pilots were seeing anti-aircraft weapons firing at them, and it became a normal event to see bullets just barely missing our airplanes. We were all seasoned veterans of this environment. To further demonstrate my mindset, I actually began to believe it was safer to land on an aircraft carrier than it was to land at a regular airport.

Bob briefed the mission as he was a LCDR and senior to my LT ranking. We both discussed the position of the anti-aircraft machine guns located at the bridge. There were four sets of them that would be firing at us. The aerial photos we had showed that there were two located on each side of the bridge, separated by the road that ran between them. There would be no planes accompanying us to attack these gun emplacements as there had been on some of the larger strikes.

Bob and I were each carrying two, one thousand-pound bombs that were set with delayed fuses, which meant they would hit the ground and detonate about a half second later. This delay was designed to have the bomb destroy the buried supports of the bridge. We decided to make two runs each so we could determine from each other's bomb hits what the wind was doing to the trajectory of the falling bombs. We knew this was somewhat risky as the gunners would be able to determine what our attack route of flight would be when we rolled in for the bomb runs.

It was a fairly clear day for Vietnam, with just a few clouds drifting over the target area as we approached it. As briefed, Bob rolled in first and surprised the ground gunners as they did not fire at him. I attacked less than a minute later, and all of the gunners opened fire on me. Bob's bomb missed to the left of the far end of the bridge. I adjusted for this situation and flew down between the gunfire and dropped one of my bombs. It missed to the right of the bridge.

Bob and I talked about the "squirrely" (changing) winds, and he made his second run. Once again, his bomb just missed the target, and he came very close to being shot down. I could see the gun sites firing at him and realized the odds of being hit increased with four gun positions shooting at you at the same time. On my next run, I assessed the wind direction and rolled in to drop my final one thousand-pound bomb. Luckily, all the bullets flying by me missed, and I dropped the bomb at about forty-five hundred feet.

It made a direct hit at the far end of the bridge and detonated shortly afterwards, causing the bridge to raise up off the supports and fall into the river. Bob and I exited the area with no further problems with enemy gun fire. We returned to the carrier and routinely briefed another mission with different pilots for later that night.

A few weeks later I received the **Distinguished Flying Cross** for my involvement with destroying the bridge.

Citation
The President of the United States takes pleasure in presenting the **Distinguished Flying Cross** *to Lieutenant Julian Harvey Harper, United States Naval Reserve.*

For heroism and extraordinary achievement while participating in aerial flight as a pilot of jet aircraft while attached to Attack

Squadron ONE HUNDRED TWELVE, embarked in USS KITTY HAWK (CVA 63) during a strike against the Chu Le Highway Bridge in North Vietnam on 22 April 1968. Skillfully maneuvering to maintain his position as wingman in poor weather conditions during a reconnaissance mission over enemy territory, Lieutenant Harper visually acquired this strategic bridge through swiftly moving clouds. He then directed the movement of the section to an attack position. After an initial attack on the bridge, target winds were revealed to be much greater than predicted and only the approach to the bridge was cratered. In spite of being tracked by enemy anti-aircraft artillery, Lieutenant Harper courageously delayed his re-attack to observe his leader's final bomb impact in order to more accurately predict wind corrections. Diving through broken clouds and severe turbulence, he delivered his remaining one thousand-pound bomb with deadly accuracy, completely destroying the bridge. Lieutenant Harper's courage, determination and superb aeronautical skill were in keeping with the highest traditions of the United States Naval Service.

For the President, John J. Hyland, Admiral, U. S. Navy, Commander in Chief U. S. Pacific Fleet."

Chapter 21
HONG KONG; FINAL LINE PERIOD; HOME

After flying another mission on May 1st, I was briefed, along with three other pilots, on taking four airplanes to Cubi Point. Having completed forty combat missions during this last line period, it was nice to be taking a break. We arrived in Cubi Point with no incidents and waited for the ship to pull into port the following day. Checking back aboard the carrier, we departed soon for Hong Kong and some well-deserved liberty.

We had less than ten days in Hong Kong, but it was wonderful to see the city all lit up at night. It was, and still is, the marketplace of the world, and during our visit, it was under the control of the British. That made it full of pomp and formality, which only the British could establish in their colonies.

Hong Kong was actually divided into two parts: Hong Kong and Kowloon. Between the two was the harbor, and it was always alive with junks, sampans, and people. Passenger liners and freighters from all parts of the world were also part of the everyday scene in Hong Kong.

Our squadron set up our admin ashore in Kowloon just as we had done during our last visit. Needless to say, without Sandy visiting me that trip, it was not nearly as much fun. We departed the harbor May 10th, as I recall, and were flying missions back on Yankee Station May 13, 1968.

Khe Sanh was still under attack by the North Vietnamese regular troops, and on May 15th and 17th, I flew missions dropping CBU-24 series weapons in support of the defense of the base. CBU stands for cluster bomb units, which were originally invented towards the end of World War II. When they were initially introduced into the Vietnam theater of operations, the planes delivering them had to fly relatively low and slow to allow the bomblets, which were similar to grenades, to be ejected out of the back of a tube that was attached to the aircraft. This method of delivery had changed by the time I arrived in Vietnam to a more normal delivery method of diving at the target at high speed and releasing the weapon. The CBU-24 we used would fall towards the ground and break open at about fifteen hundred feet, dispersing hundreds of steel, ball-filled bomblets. They were called "guavas" by the North Vietnamese troops as they looked like the fruit. One bomb could cover an area approximately three hundred by one thousand yards, making it a great weapon to use for flak suppression missions and troops positioned in a line, which was the situation in the Khe Sanh area.

It was too small to do much damage to trucks or equipment, but it had devastating effects on enemy troops. Fortunately for using them in our applications, there were no civilians or any other non-combatants in the area on the enemy side of the firing line around Khe Sanh. I understand that at a later date, following the Vietnam War, there were restrictions placed on where and how they could be used.

After delivering these weapons, we would circle back around to the North Vietnamese firing line and strafe the jungle area, trying to keep the troops pinned down and away from the base. As mentioned earlier, we carried eighty rounds of 20mm as a standard load on the A-4. This was to be used in the event a crew was shot down and we needed to keep the enemy away while the helicopter was coming in to pick them up.

During the defense of Khe Sanh, we changed this procedure. After delivering my primary weapons during this siege, including bombs, rockets, and napalm on the enemy, I emptied all eight rounds of 20mm bullets that were on my airplane, which we had normally saved for rescue work. These dates were January 21st, March 9th, and 11th, May 13th, 18th, and 22nd. On March 7th, I was armed with a Gatlin gun, and after making several runs against the North Vietnamese positions around the base, I expended 1,490 rounds of 20mm bullets. I'm certain these attacks helped to keep them from overrunning our base.

Mission number 198 was a night flight over North Vietnam to find and destroy trucks. I was awarded a **Gold Star in lieu of a Second Navy Achievement Medal** for my actions on that flight.

Citation

For meritorious achievement as a pilot of jet aircraft while attached to Attack Squadron ONE HUNDRED TWELVE embarked in USS KITTY HAWK (CVA-63). On 26 May 1968, Lieutenant Harper was the wingman on a night reconnaissance mission over North Vietnam. Arriving over enemy territory, he quickly located a lone enemy truck which he destroyed through a precise bombing attack. Moving deeper into enemy territory, a convoy of trucks was located and immediately attacked, causing three of the trucks to explode and burst into flames. As he recovered from his dive bombing run, accurate antiaircraft fire was directed at his aircraft. While maneuvering to avoid this threat, he expertly repositioned his aircraft and reattacked the blazing column of trucks, once again scoring direct hits in spite of the artillery fire which bracketed his aircraft. Lieutenant HARPER's superior airmanship and loyal devotion to duty reflected great credit upon himself and were in keeping with the highest traditions of the United States Naval Service. Lieutenant HARPER is authorized to wear the Combat "V."

For the Secretary, W. F. Bringle, Vice Admiral, United States Navy.

Earlier in May, I had advised the Navy Bureau of Personnel that I would not be accepting their offer of becoming a regular officer in the US Navy. The two combat cruises back to back were beginning to take their toll on me. To say that I had become insensitive on many issues of combat would be an understatement. Watching planes being hit and sometimes destroyed right in front of you was an indescribable experience, yet this was a common occurrence over North Vietnam. Hearing professional aviators crying over the radio as they were attacked and hearing planes being shot down by MIG fighter jets was hard to take.

Being away from home with my wife expecting our first child was also very difficult to accept. I remembered joining VA-112 in the Mediterranean as a replacement for one of the naval aviators who had been killed while landing on the carrier. We lost three pilots on that cruise and were not involved in any combat operations. Naval aviation is by design very dangerous, and I thought that my one tour of duty was enough. I elected to stay as a USNR Officer and leave after my first tour of duty.

I received orders that after our squadron arrived in Lemoore and I had helped to train my replacement, I would be transferring to VA-127. It was an instrument training squadron flying the T-A4 Skyhawk, and I would stay there to finish my tour of active service in the navy (just under five years). Another squadron mate, LCDR Jim Lucchesi, would also be joining the training squadron after I arrived there. Unfortunately, a short while after Jim joined VA-127, he along with his student, were killed on a training mission over the Sierra Nevada mountain range.

June 1st arrived, and I was scheduled to fly my last two missions at night as we were operating on a red carrier schedule (midnight to noon). I attended the briefing for the first of the two missions, only to find out the weather was so bad it had to be cancelled. I had the same luck on the second mission, which was also at night. I went back to my stateroom disappointed as I needed those two missions to obtain two hundred combat flights.

Shortly after I went to sleep, my roommate Bob Saville arrived in the room and woke me up and offered me his two missions. He had previously reached the two hundred combat flight mark and knew I wanted to obtain that number also. As a warrior, I enthusiastically accepted his offer and attended the first briefing. The weather cleared up enough to fly, and by this time, it was a daylight flight that went off without a hitch.

After I arrived back on the carrier, I went straight down to the ready room and took part in the next briefing. It was to be a flight of four A-4s with me flying the number four position. We were to fly down south below the DMZ to meet a forward air controller (FAC). He would assign us a target located on the Ho Chi Minh Trail. It seemed quite fitting to be mission number 200 bombing the Ho Chi Minh Trail as we had done so many times before.

After our planes arrived in the pre-briefed area, we contacted the FAC, and he told us he had a target for us to bomb. All of us in our flight were carrying MK 82 five hundred-pound bombs. The target was described to our flight as a convoy of trucks headed south under all the jungle foliage on the Ho Chi Minh Trail. Since it was our last mission, we had all agreed that we would only be making one run and getting our flight back to the carrier in one piece! After the three planes ahead of me completed their dive runs, I rolled in and dropped my bombs on the target area. Once again, I thought I was just making tooth picks out of trees as I could not see anything but the smoke from the FAC marking flare.

As I pulled off this final run to climb back to altitude and join the rest of my flight, the FAC ask our flight leader if we had any 20mm left. He said he had several elephants that had run off the trail and were in the open. Our flight leader responded that he would have to get the next group of pilots to strafe the elephants as we had just completed our final combat run of the war. The FAC congratulated all of us, and we changed radio frequencies to continue back to the carrier.

I remember thinking to myself, *I've never had an interest to kill elephants—although I'm sure I did when bombing the Ho Chi Minh Trail.* I found that thought interesting as I certainly didn't mind killing enemy troops. Combat really changes your perception of things.

For our squadron, the air war was over for this cruise. VA-112 would come back to Vietnam for one more cruise before being disbanded. Leaving Yankee Station, this quote appeared in our ship's cruise book from General William C. Westmoreland, who was the Commander, Allied Forces Vietnam:

On the occasion of the departure from Vietnam water of Kitty Hawk, I wish to convey to this fine fighting team my appreciation for their outstanding support. Her aircraft have flown numerous sorties in defense of the Khe Sanh and surrounding areas. Particular note is also made of Kitty Hawk's having **completed 61 days** on the line, a record for the Vietnam conflict. My congratulations to all concerned.

Another short quote from our cruise book concerning our involvement in Vietnam was from Vice Admiral William F. Bringle, Commander, US Seventh Fleet:

> Of all the units of the Seventh Fleet, Kitty Hawk has been called upon to operate the **longest** under the most demanding conditions. You have provided valuable assistance to our ground forces in the northern 1ˢᵗ Corps and maintained unrelenting pressure on the enemy. I wish to express my admiration for your spirit, hard work and self-sacrifice.

The day after I finished my last mission, I caught a twin engine carrier on-board delivery (COD) plane and flew over to Clark Air Force Base in the Philippines. This had been planned as the skipper knew I wanted to get home and meet my new daughter, who had been born on May 21, 1968.

When I reached Clark Air Force Base, the line to sign up for a flight home was very long. I would estimate the number of military personnel standing in the line to be at least several hundred. I'm sure it would have taken me days to arrange for a flight back to the states. I found out where Flight Operations was located and went there to see if I could find another way to get to the states. I wasn't having much luck until an air force captain, after hearing my story that I was telling the operation's officer, came up to me and said I could ride the jump seat in the cockpit of his C-141 transport plane if I wanted to. Of course, I jumped at the opportunity.

During the long flight over the Pacific Ocean, the captain explained many of the instruments in the cockpit of the C-141 to me. Most of them were completely different than the instruments I was used to seeing in my little A-4. I distinctly remember the tape rpm gauges in his plane. As power was added to the four engines on the C-141, the tape gauges rose to indicate the number of rpms the engines were achieving. These tape gauges made it easy to spool all four engines up at the same time. You just matched the four tape gauges, and the rpms were almost the same. Years later, while I was flying the DC-10, several of the planes had the same type of tape gauges. I had a very enjoyable flight to Travis Air Force Base, located in California. As a result of the air force captain giving me a ride, later when I worked for the airlines, I allowed many qualified "stranded" people to ride in the cockpit jump seat, situated right behind my captain seat, in order for them to get home.

From Travis Air Force Base, I managed to get a flight to Lemoore, where I met my newborn daughter and reunited with Sandy.

CONCLUSION

t was hard to believe that the combat phase of my career was over. But in the true military tradition, I met my replacement, John Shaw, and flew numerous training missions with him around the Lemoore area. Thinking back about my experiences when I had first joined the squadron, I decided to continue the tradition of taking advantage of a new squadron aviator.

I briefed a training mission with John, who had heard of my air-to-air hassling skills. We were to take off from Lemoore and climb to twenty thousand feet, flying into the acrobatic area over the Sierra Nevada mountain range. There we would commence our air-to-air work. I instructed John to lead the flight, and I would be his wingman, flying in the number two position.

As soon as we took off and I retracted the aircraft's gear and flaps, I began to dump my fuel. Because I was behind John's aircraft, he could not see the fuel being dumped from my airplane. The A-4 carried a little over five thousand pounds of jet fuel, making it sluggish until you used up some of the fuel. By the time we reached the acrobatic area, my A-4 was much lighter than John's plane. We began our first hassle match, with me being able to turn more quickly, climb faster, and basically out maneuver John's plane due to the weight difference.

I quickly defeated him, and we began a new hassle experience with the same result. John asked to have one more try at defeating me. Even if I had wanted to, I said it was time to return to Lemoore Naval Air Station. John did not know my low fuel warning light was illuminating, and I knew I had to get my jet on the ground fast. We made it back and landed safely, with John telling his fellow squadron mates how good I was at hassling. I never told him about what I had done.

On another day, we took a cross-country trip over to Buckley Air Force Base just outside of Denver, in Aurora, Colorado. After refueling, we returned to Lemoore, flying at low level for much of the way. We saw several trains, and I demonstrated how to "attack" them. He was a really nice guy and was looking forward to going to Vietnam, which was rare. Unfortunately, during his first month on Yankee Station in 1969, he was killed due to a "cold cat shot" off the carrier. A cold cat shot occurs when there is not enough end speed generated by the catapult system to allow the aircraft to fly. The plane just crashes into the sea, and, most often, there is not enough time for the pilot to eject successfully.

After VA-112 returned to Lemoore, following their cruise to Vietnam, they were disbanded on October 10, 1969, bringing an end to a great attack squadron.

Sandy, our daughter, Melissa, and myself left the navy and the Lemoore Naval Air Station on December 5, 1968. We moved to the Los Angeles area where I went to work for Continental Airlines on December 7, 1968. Our second daughter, Michelle, was born on April 7, 1970.

One of my first flights as a second officer with Continental was to fly overseas to Vietnam delivering troops and ammunition to Danang. We were on final approach to the runway there when the tower called on the radio and advised us there had been reported machine gun fire close to the airport. After acknowledging their transmission, the captain was looking inside the cockpit at his instruments. The first officer and I were looking out the front window of the Boeing 707-320C. Suddenly, the airplane was covered with anti-aircraft machine gun fire. The tracers were all around us, and the first officer screamed. I calmly continued to look forward out the window thinking, *It will always be this way, bullets all around me.* I felt right at home and at total ease.

After thirty-five years of flying for Continental Airlines, I retired with over thirty-three thousand flight hours flying the Boeing 707-320C, the Boeing 727, the McDonnell Douglas DC-10, and, finally, the Boeing 777. I never had damage done to any of these airplanes during all of my flying hours aboard them.

After my retirement, people have asked me if I miss flying. I tell them I miss the camaraderie of the airline's crews and flying to different cities and countries. I miss the thrill of combat and flying to outmaneuver the SAMs and machine gun fire. I miss surviving circumstances that could just as easily have cost my life. When I look up and see a military jet, I always think about the pilot having complete freedom and experiencing things that cannot be duplicated down here on earth. I miss my military pilot friends whose lives were cut short by accidents and war. Someday I hope to continue my cruise with them.

Not bad for starting with a sixty-three-cent flight! To the best of my knowledge, I have never been shot at again.

SUPER 8 MOVIE AVAILABLE

Bringing the War to the Enemy is a *home movie* edited from over two thousand feet of super 8 movie film that I took while flying missions over Vietnam. It runs a little over sixteen minutes in duration and documents typical combat missions we flew daily during my two cruises aboard the USS Kitty Hawk from 1966–1968. It has scenes taken in the ready room, on the flight deck, and inside the cockpit, showing take offs and landings on-board the carrier. It also shows flying scenes approaching North Vietnam on an actual bombing mission and visually displays much of what the book has discussed in detail.

In addition, it shows a Bullpup missile being launched and guided by me to the target, complete with pictures taken afterwards of the destroyed bridge. One of the high points in the film is when a SAM comes directly in front of the airplane, complete with the original soundtrack that gave me the warning a missile had been launched and was tracking me.

It shows many flying scenes, including air-to-air refueling and formation flying, and it concludes with landing on the carrier.

If you are interested in obtaining a copyrighted version of this film, please visit my website: www.Juleshharper.com.

A free eBook edition is available with the purchase of this book.

To claim your free eBook edition:

1. Download the Shelfie app.
2. Write your name in uppser case in the box.
3. Use the Shelfie app to submit a photo.
4. Download your eBook to any device.

Shelfie

A free eBook edition is available
with the purchase of this print book.

CLEARLY PRINT YOUR NAME ABOVE IN UPPER CASE

Instructions to claim your free eBook edition:
1. Download the Shelfie app for Android or iOS
2. Write your name in **UPPER CASE** above
3. Use the Shelfie app to submit a photo
4. Download your eBook to any device

Print & Digital Together Forever.

Snap a photo

Free eBook

Read anywhere

The Morgan James
Speakers Group

↑ www.TheMorganJamesSpeakersGroup.com

We connect Morgan James published authors with live and online events and audiences whom will benefit from their expertise.

 Morgan James makes all of our titles available
through the Library for All Charity Organization.

www.LibraryForAll.org